Intelligent
Influence

Intelligent Influence

The 4 Steps of Highly Successful Leaders and Organizations

by

DALE G. CALDWELL

Published by Intelligent Influence Publishing Group,
an imprint of Intelligent Influence, Inc.
www.IntelligentInfluenceInc.com

Book design by Pine Orchard, Inc.
www.pineorchard.com

Printed in USA

EAN (ISBN-13): 978-0983896395
Library of Congress Card Number: 2012951547

Dale G. Caldwell

Dale is motivated by his passion for understanding the fundamental ingredients of both individual and organizational success. As the CEO (or President) of nine organizations in the public, private, and nonprofit/civic sectors over the last 25 years, he learned how to strategically utilize influence to achieve extraordinary success. In this exceptionally entertaining and thought-provoking book, Dale explains how his ground-breaking *Intelligent Influence* process is the foundation of success in business and life. He opens readers minds to the reality that they "*do what they do, think the way they think, and accomplish what they accomplish because of influence.*"

Dale is the CEO of the management consulting firm Strategic Influence which uses his *Intelligent Influence* competency framework to provide strategy, operations, and human capital consulting advice to corporations, government agencies, and nonprofits around the world. He received a BA in Economics from Princeton University and a MBA in Finance from the Wharton School of the University of Pennsylvania. Dale also completed the Harvard Kennedy School Senior Executives in State and Local Government program.

He is the author of three books and a member of the Board of Directors of the United States Tennis Association (USTA). Dale is an accomplished athlete who has completed three marathons and received national rankings in tennis, triathlon, and duathlon. He lives in New Jersey with his wife Sharon and daughter Ashley.

Other books by Dale G. Caldwell:

School To Work To Success

Tennis in New York

Fruit of the Spirit Poems and Hymns

DEDICATION

This book is dedicated to my wife Sharon
Marie Caldwell; my daughter Ashley
Marie Caldwell; my mother Grace Estelle
Dungee Caldwell; my father Reverend
Gilbert Haven Caldwell, Jr.; and my
brother Paul Douglass Caldwell.

They have each played a vitally important
role in teaching me that influence is the
key to success in any endeavor involving
human interaction.

Table of Contents

ACKNOWLEDGMENTS

I have been influenced in many positive ways by the wonderful family members, friends, co-workers, and bosses that have enhanced my life over the last 50 years. I also learned a great deal from the people and events that have been negative influences in my life. I feel blessed that the combination of these influences has given me the insight to develop a new way to strategically use influence to achieve personal and professional success.

I am among a fortunate group of business leaders who have held some very interesting senior leadership positions in the public, private, and nonprofit/civic sectors. These positions, in combination with my passion for research, have given me unique insight into the patterns of both successful and failed businesses and leaders. *Intelligent Influence: The 4 Steps of Highly Successful Leaders and Organizations* describes, in a fascinating and unique way, the influence-based patterns of success of extraordinary businesses and their leaders. It is based both on my research and my successes and failures as a student, new employee, human resources executive, nonprofit leader, government official, financial planner, real estate executive, management consultant, board member, and chief executive officer (CEO). Each chapter of this book is a compilation of the many lessons about influence in life and business that I have learned from my research and personal journey.

I will never be able to thank everyone who has taught me important life and career lessons over the years. However, in the next few paragraphs, I would like to acknowledge just a few of the people who have played an important role in helping me understand influence.

I must begin these acknowledgments by thanking my wife Sharon and daughter Ashley for their support in the development of this book. Their love, patience, and guidance helped to make this book possible. I am eternally grateful to my wonderful parents Reverend Gilbert Caldwell (a retired United Methodist minister) and Grace Dungee Caldwell (a retired schoolteacher). I cannot imagine having better parents. They were able to influence my brother Paul and me to believe that, if we worked hard enough, we could accomplish anything that we wanted to in life. This belief has been the foundation of my life and the reason why I truly believe that this little book on influence can start a movement that will change the way in which people throughout the world interact with each other.

I am also grateful to my brother Paul who has been a successful engineer with several of the largest aerospace engineering companies in the world. As his older brother, I forced him to be the first victim of my many attempts to influence. I am grateful to him for putting up with a bothersome older brother and always being there to support me.

I have had the benefit of working with leaders in many different industries that taught me some amazing lessons about the role of influence in business success and failure. I am fortunate that my boss at Quaker Oats (my first full-time job after college) gave me my first business lesson on negative influence. Thanks to him, I learned early in my career that success in the world of work is not based on merit. In addition, I owe my co-workers at the Wharton Small Business Development Center (SBDC) a debt of gratitude for influencing me to spend much of my professional life as a management consultant.

I am grateful to all my bosses and co-workers at Deloitte Consulting who helped me sharpen my analytical skills and taught me how to work hard and smart. I extend a special thanks to my first and last management consulting boss Ed Ruzinsky who has had a legendary career in multiple businesses. His incredibly calm and positive approach to the stress of business has been a great inspiration. I owe a professional debt to Marc Schwarz who took a chance on hiring me when I was a young inexperienced Wharton MBA student. Marc's intense focus on business and willingness to make me uncomfortable (in a very positive way) helped to push me to get the most out of my professional skills.

I am extremely grateful to John DiMaggio who made consulting fun and was the sponsor behind many of my promotions and raises over the years.

I am also thankful that I had the great pleasure of working with Jim Wall, Paul Gallagher, and Jack Beighley. These outstanding human resources professionals taught me how to recruit, train, and develop employees. I am especially grateful to Tim Washington and Dexter Bridgeman for partnering with me in the development of some very successful career and life mentoring programs that have positively influenced young people in many countries around the world.

I am thankful to the entire board of the Newark Alliance for hiring me to be the first Executive Director of what was arguably the most influential nonprofit organization in New Jersey. In this role, I learned a great deal about the power of individual and organizational influence. I am particularly grateful to these bosses: former New Jersey Governor Thomas H. Kean for teaching me how important compassionate leadership is to success; philanthropist Ray Chambers for teaching me how important mental and physical health is to impactful leadership; and Prudential Financial CEO Art Ryan for demonstrating that you can be an incredibly successful corporate CEO and have a passionate interest in helping local communities at the same time.

I am grateful to former New Jersey Department of Community Affairs (DCA) Commissioner Susan Bass Levin for teaching me that the key to success in the public sector is being honest and working harder than anyone else. It was a great honor working with Heather Allen, Ethel Winckler, and Suzanne Winderman who, as executive assistants, had extraordinary influence which they used to help me become successful. Their guidance and support through many challenging aspects of my career have been a blessing.

Finally, I would like to thank my friends Christian Benedetto, Janet Granger, Dina Lichtman, Terry McCarthy, Nish and Hetal Parikh, and Deepak Trivedi for doing a phenomenal job of communicating the value and power of *Intelligent Influence* to hundreds of businesses around the world. They were early believers in this concept and initiated the process of changing the way that the business world views the connection between influence and success. Their support and guidance has meant more to me than they will ever know.

Why Intelligent Influence?

Econ 101

Like many management consultants, I have spent my entire career attempting to identify the common best practices that have enabled companies like Coca-Cola, Disney, Johnson & Johnson, and Nike to achieve extraordinary success. Many books have attempted to be the first to uncover the secrets of legendary businesses and their leaders. Some of the best business writers in history have developed excellent theories about business management and corporate profitability.

I have read many of the best business books ever written. In reviewing these well-crafted publications, I was surprised to discover that none of these books provided an extensive analysis of the foundation of sustainable business and professional success. They overlooked the powerful role of "influence" in business profitability and productivity. Some writers ignored the connection between influence and success. Other authors mention influence, in passing, without providing a well-thought-out strategy for maximizing influence. I wrote *Intelligent Influence: The 4 Steps of Highly Successful Leaders and Organizations* to fill this void in business strategy.

There are some very good books about sales and influence. However, *Intelligent Influence* is the first book to identify the influence-driven process that is the single most important factor in the success of organizations and leaders. The framework, presented in the pages that follow, provides a road map on the strategic use of influence that promises to transform the way that executives and scholars look at business leadership.

My fascination with the subject of extraordinary business success was inspired by one of my first classes at Princeton University. I remember sitting in the large lecture hall on the very first day of Economics 101 thinking how exciting it was that someone like me (who had grown up in poor urban communities in Boston and New York) had a chance to attend one of the best universities in the world. However, my excitement quickly turned to boredom when I discovered that the focus of this class was on the theory of economics, not the application of this discipline in the real world. I remember wishing that I could find a business course (Business Success 101) that would teach me the foundation of success in the business world. Unfortunately, no course of this type existed at Princeton or any other university. I grew to appreciate the value of theoretical thinking and went on to major in economics. However, I always dreamed of developing a course that covered the secrets of business success in an entertaining and practical way.

In many ways, *Intelligent Influence: The 4 Steps of Highly Successful Leaders and Organizations* is the course that I dreamed about, condensed into an easy-to-read book. It took me 30 years (and executive positions in management consulting, finance, education, government, real estate, and sports) to develop and write. However, this book is the first publication to provide insight into the influence-driven process that successful corporations and executives have utilized (consciously or subconsciously) to achieve extraordinary business goals. People reading this book, in its entirety, will understand the critical role that the strategic management of influence has on their professional success and the profitability of their company.

I have had the wonderful opportunity to present the *Intelligent Influence* framework to thousands of men and women over the last few years. I continue to be amazed at the way that this concept has changed the manner in which my audiences approach their business and life. I wrote this book to build on these presentations and transform the way in which readers intelligently utilize influence to achieve their personal and professional goals. It is important to note that this is the first book in a series of books on *Intelligent Influence* (i^2). I am currently writing several other books that explain how the *Intelligent Influence* process is the foundation of success in areas as diverse as internet marketing, relationships, parenting, education, government, nonprofits, religion, and sports.

Since this publication is presenting a radically different view of extraordinary leadership in business, it is intended to be an interesting introduction to a very unique four-step process. I present a new language around the elusive concept of influence. Readers will find themselves thinking very differently about human interaction. They will likely find real value in reviewing sections of the book independently. I have, therefore, repeated definitions throughout the book so that readers can review each of the chapters in Sections I, II, III, and IV independently.

Hidden in Plain Sight

Amazingly, the word "influence" is "hidden in plain sight" in the language of today's complex business world. The word is used, by millions of business people, on a daily basis without a comprehensive understanding of the vitally important role that influence plays in the success or failure of their organization. Virtually everyone uses the word. However, few people understand that influence is the primary reason why they *do what they do and think the way they think.*

Tragically, most executives have no idea how to intentionally use influence to increase the profitability of their business, expand market share, or get a promotion. The strategic use of influence is the foundation of individual and organizational success. Corporations seeking to exceed productivity and profitability goals must develop business strategies focused on maximizing their influence in the marketplace.

The success or failure of a product is proportionate to the influence it has on consumers. The productivity of employees, at every level of an organization, is directly related to the amount of influence they have on their peers, subordinates, and supervisors. The use of influence in strategic ways can significantly increase market share; improve organizational efficiency; lead to the effective development of exceptional leaders; increase the engagement and retention of staff; and assess, in unique ways, the talent of current and future employees.

Intelligent Influence

The seamless interconnection of dynamic global economies in today's business world has challenged leaders to develop new approaches to deal with constant global change. Far too many companies are struggling in today's business environment because of poor leadership strategies. Traditional theories of leadership have not provided senior executives with the tools they need to address the rapidly changing world of commerce (especially in a challenging international economic climate).

The globalization of the business world (combined with the rapid increase in the skill, experience, racial, cultural, and ethnic diversity of corporate employees) has made the "command and control" leadership styles of the past impotent. Leaders, in most corporations, can no longer order people around successfully. They have to influence their subordinates in a way that will transform them into high-potential employees. Gone are the days when executives can give the proverbial order to their employees to "jump" and the employees say "how high?" In today's business world, when a leader asks a subordinate to do the proverbial jump, the employee will ask: "Why?" or "What do I get out of jumping?" or possibly, "I'm busy. Why don't you jump?"

The successful leaders of today are sensitive to the influences affecting employee performance. They recognize that commanding people to do things limits their effectiveness, creativity, and engagement with the company. They utilize a leadership style, based on the strategic use of influence, that motivates others to achieve peak performance. The discovery of this cataclysmic change in effective leadership styles inspired me to develop a new approach to individual and organizational success that I call "*Intelligent Influence.*"

This trademarked revolutionary new formula for human interaction provides a framework that explains how individuals or organizations can enhance their effectiveness and success by managing how they are both influencing others and being influenced. I define *Intelligent Influence* as "*a learned competency that, without exertion of force or direct exercise of command, produces an effect that leads to extraordinary results driven by effective human interaction.*" In short, *Intelligent Influence* provides a proven step-by-step approach to increasing a person's professional success or an organization's profitability.

Armed with knowledge about how people have been influenced and how they intelligently influence others, executives and managers can approach problems and challenging situations more effectively. Insight into how these leaders have been influenced and how they influence others enable them to maximize their effectiveness as leaders within any organization that requires significant human interaction. The *Intelligent Influence* process helps individuals value the influence-based differences of their peers, subordinates, and supervisors in a way that increases their engagement and effectiveness within the organization.

This unique approach to influence also applies to corporations. Regardless of how they are formed, why they come together, and for how long, all effective organizations need to learn how to manage their internal influences and maximize their external influences to achieve their goals. All successful corporations understand how to manage their internal influences in a way that will enable them to have the external influence they need to maximize sales and profitability. The *Intelligent Influence* process provides a unique influence-based strategic approach that will increase the success of corporations of any size in any industry.

The Power of Influence

My introduction to the power of influence came more than 25 years ago in South Africa when, during apartheid (a rule of law that prohibited citizens of different races from living in the same neighborhoods or attending the same schools), I stayed in the home of the former white South African ambassador to Bolivia. I was the only African-American on the trip. However, because I was an American, I received a special approval from the government to stay in the home of a white South African.

When I arrived at the ambassador's house in the early evening, I was dressed in jeans and a t-shirt because I wanted to be comfortable on the long trip from Zimbabwe. That night I had a chance to interact extensively with the ambassador, his wife, and their 7-year-old daughter. I wore a suit the next morning because I had a business meeting in Johannesburg. At the breakfast table, their beautiful daughter looked me up and down, turned to her parents, and surprised us all by saying: *"You know, black Americans aren't any different than white South Africans!"*

In an instant, I saw the role of influence in the country's public policy. For decades, young white South Africans were influenced to think that blacks were inferior. Black residents of the country were not allowed to hold leadership positions of any type (except in black-only areas). As a result, young whites were influenced to believe that black Africans were incapable of doing what whites could do. They were trained to view most black people as intellectually inferior individuals who could clean an office but never manage it. This influence led to inhuman racial discrimination and the murder of thousands of black South Africans who had the audacity to believe that they deserved the same rights as white residents.

This insightful young girl taught me the power of positive influence. I discovered that the right kind of influence, at the right time, can change the views of one person and, potentially, the world. However, it took me more than 25 years of experience (as a senior executive in the public, private, and civic/nonprofit sectors) and extensive research on leadership to realize that influence is the foundation of business and individual success. Like most people in leadership roles, I was so fascinated with the concept of exceptional leadership that I overlooked the incredible power of influence. I wrote *Intelligent Influence: The 4 Steps of Highly Successful Leaders and Organizations* to show, through the proven success of executives and companies, that influence is the foundation of successful leadership.

Studying Leadership

I first developed a passion for leadership at a very young age. When I was a child, all my heroes were famous people who were leaders in their respective endeavors. I was mesmerized by iconic individuals like Arthur Ashe; Lew Alcindor (who became Kareem Abdul Jabbar); Cassius Clay (who became Muhammad Ali); Thomas Edison; Henry Ford; Mahatma Gandhi; John F. Kennedy; Dr. Martin Luther King, Jr.; John D. Rockefeller; Franklin D. Roosevelt; and others who used very different styles to lead very diverse groups of people toward extremely difficult goals. I was fascinated by their success. However, at that time in my life, I could not understand why some people, holding leadership positions, succeeded and others failed.

I learned a great deal more about leadership later in life because I had the honor of serving as the President and/or Chief Executive Officer (CEO) of nine organizations (two, for-profit; three, government; and four, nonprofit). These positions convinced me that leadership is one of the most important and least understood subjects in the world. Leadership plays a vitally important role in every aspect of human society and life. Health, education, the environment, religion, science, business, government, nonprofits, families, and basic human interaction are all directly affected by leadership in one way or another.

Effective leaders can improve the quality of life for every human being on earth while ineffective or unethical leaders can create global chaos. Since the right leader can inspire followers to cure disease, eradicate poverty, sustain the environment, increase employment, eliminate illiteracy, reduce crime, and bring about global peace, it is essential—for the good of humanity—to understand the foundation of successful leadership.

Several years ago, I began the process of learning as much as I could about leadership. I read many books and papers on the subject, observed leaders at all levels of society, and immersed myself in the research of a great variety of organizations dedicated to the study of leadership or the training of leaders. My goal was to figure out what makes a leader successful. To my surprise, this analysis taught me much more about success in life than I ever imagined it could. In my research, I uncovered some amazing secrets about leadership and successful human interaction.

I have always been fascinated by word definitions. In my review of the definitions of common leadership terms, I was surprised to discover that one word connected many of the traditional definitions of leadership. Merriam-Webster's Dictionary defines a *"leader"* as *"a person who has commanding authority or influence."* *"Authority"* is defined as *"power to influence or command thought, opinion, or behavior."* *"Command"* is defined as *"exercising a dominating influence over."* Since a person's *authority* and ability to *command* is driven by *influence*, it is logical to conclude that the relative success of a *leader* is determined by the extent of their influence over others. In other words: *Leadership is driven by influence.*

Merriam-Webster's Dictionary defines the word *"influence"* as *"the act or power of producing an effect without apparent exertion of force or direct exercise of command.*" This definition forced me to examine whether influence was more than the foundation of leadership. I, therefore, spent a great deal of time studying the role of influence both on the world and in my life.

In doing this research, I learned how important influence was to the lives of every person on earth. Influence "produced" many of the most important "effects" both in everyday activities and major human events. *We all do what we do and think the way we think because of influence.* Our favorite foods, sports teams, and recreational activities are guided by the unique influences in our lives. Our political views, the people we find attractive, our language and accent are all dictated by the influences in our lives. I was surprised to learn that the success or failure of corporations or business leaders was also rooted in influence.

There is an amazing amount of research on leadership. However, I was extremely surprised to discover that, in spite of the incredible power of influence on every aspect of human life, there was little substantive targeted research on the specific role of influence on daily life and major historical events. I decided that I would become one of the first people to focus my research on "influence as the foundation of leadership" instead of "leadership as the foundation of influence" as others had done.

Influence in Business

One of my favorite influence quotes is from Friedrich Nietzsche. This 19th century philosopher said: "*The future influences the present just as much as the past.*" Modern technology provides the historical data necessary for today's executives to develop comprehensive plans for the future of their business. As described by Nietzsche more than 150 years ago, these future plans not only have a direct influence on current business operations, they also impact how employees need to leverage past business and personal influences for future success.

The strategic use of influence is the foundation of individual and organizational success. The productivity of employees, at every level of an organization, is directly correlated with the influence they have on their peers, subordinates, and supervisors. Corporations, seeking to exceed productivity and profitability goals, must develop business strategies focused on maximizing their influence in the marketplace.

The *Intelligent Influence* process provides the guidance business, government and nonprofit leaders need to enhance both their careers and the effectiveness of their organizations in today's fast-paced business environment. This unique approach to organizational leadership will transform the way in which executives approach success and in which corporations pursue increased productivity and profitability.

One of the most fascinating things about this new framework is how it explains the reasons why the best-known executives and companies succeed in very competitive marketplaces. *Intelligent Influence: The 4 Steps of Highly Successful Leaders and Organizations* will explore some of the most fascinating stories of business success in the context of the *Intelligent Influence* framework. This revolutionary new business approach, rooted in the strategic use of influence, is identified by the following trademarked symbol:

Intelligent Influence Framework

If applied correctly, the strategic use of influence will not only help individuals increase their professional success, it will enable any organization of any size to maximize sales; improve operational efficiency; develop exceptional leaders; increase the engagement and retention of employees; assess the talent of current and future employees; and maximize the effectiveness of a diverse workforce. The foundation of this new approach to success is the *Intelligent Influence Framework*[TM] which contains the following eight components:

- *Internal Influence™*
- *Exernal Influence™*
- *Influence Understanding™*
- *Influence Actions™*
- *Influence Awareness™*
- *Influence Impact™*
- *Influence Management™*
- *Influence Maximization™*

The *Intelligent Influence Framework* is illustrated in the following diagram:

Intelligent Influence Framework™

	Internal Influence	External Influence
Influence Understanding	Step 1 **Influence Awareness**	Step 2 **Influence Impact**
Influence Actions	Step 3 **Influence Management**	Step 4 **Influence Maximization**

This diagram recurs throughout the chapters for convenient referral. Each of the four boxes depicts a step in the *Intelligent Influence* process that we consider to be an "*Influence Competence™*." These steps (or competences) are based on a learned capacity rooted in *Intelligent Influence* that, in combination, results in outstanding performance in any endeavor that requires significant human interaction. These four steps are the secret of success of extraordinary individuals and organizations. This comprehensive approach to organizational improvement is based on enhancing the internal and external influences of both employees and organizations in a way that will help them maximize their effectiveness in business.

Intelligent Influence is more important than Intelligence Quotient (IQ) or Emotional Intelligence (EI) in determining performance because success or failure, in work and life, is determined largely by the type of influence individuals have on the people they interact with on a regular basis. This framework is also the foundation of organization and team success. If utilized effectively, *Intelligent Influence* will help individuals and organizations identify important developmental needs that will enable them to make the adjustments necessary to increase their probability of success in any endeavor involving human interaction.

Internal Influence

The steps in the *Intelligent Influence Framework* can be divided into two categories related to the internal or external impact of influence. The first category is called *Internal Influence*. The steps in this category include *Influence Awareness* and *Influence Management* and refer to the ways in which individuals or organizations have been influenced or are managing the ways in which they are influenced.

External Influence

The second category is called *External Influence*. The steps in this category include *Influence Impact* and *Influence Maximization* and refer to individuals or organizations becoming aware of their current influence or maximizing the influence they have on others. This type of influence is focused on the external branding of a person, an organization, or a product. It represents the way in which a person influences others or the manner in which a business influences employees and customers.

Influence Understanding

The steps or competencies in the *Intelligent Influence Framework* can also be divided into two categories related to the development of an understanding of influence or taking action on influence. The first of these categories is called *Influence Understanding*. The steps in this category include *Influence Awareness* and *Influence Impact* and refer to the effort of individuals and organizations to understand how they have been influenced or how they influence others. It is essential for any company and individual to assess the ways in which they have been influenced in business and the manner in which they are currently influencing others.

Influence Actions

The second of these categories is called *Influence Actions*. The steps and competencies in this category include *Influence Management* and *Influence Maximization* and refer to actions taken by individuals or organizations to manage how they are influenced to achieve a particular goal or how they maximize their influence on others.

The Secret of Business and Life Success

Throughout *Intelligent Influence: The 4 Steps of Highly Successful Leaders and Organizations*, I examine the extraordinary achievements of executives and companies in the context of *Intelligent Influence*. Amazingly, the success of these leaders and organizations is directly related to the ways in which they adhered to this framework. In Section I of the book, I describe in detail each of the four steps in the *Intelligent Influence* process.

In Section II of the book, I explain the relationship between three of the major technical business disciplines (Strategic Planning, Advertising, and Public Relations) and organizational success. In each of these three chapters, I provide a business case that demonstrates how the *Intelligent Influence* approach was the secret to their extraordinary success.

In Section III of the book, I explain the relationship between three of the major people business disciplines (Leadership, Sales, and Diversity) and individual success. In each of these three chapters, I examine the human capital side of business by using the four-step *Intelligent Influence* process to explain individual business success.

Finally, in Section IV of the book, I provide useful exercises designed to help readers increase their *Intelligent Influence Quotient*^{TM} (IIQ). As readers work through these exercises, they will likely notice that the unique approach to human interaction presented in *Intelligent Influence* is applicable to areas outside of business. From parenting to politics, from houses of worship and sports arenas to the halls of government, *Intelligent Influence* promises to rewrite the rules of how we communicate and move each other to change the world. This book is focused on the strategic use of influence in business. However, I encourage readers to consider ways in which the *Intelligent Influence* process applies to both their business and personal lives.

SECTION I

The Influence Framework

CHAPTER 1

Influence Awareness:
Clairol

Malcolm Gladwell

In today's business world, corporate offices, stores, and showrooms are more likely than ever to have four generations of workers, foreign-born employees, and a higher percentage of women and minorities. The modern international, multi-generational, and multi-racial business environment requires leaders to have the ability to understand the needs, wants, desires, and struggles of people who are very different than they are. This unique insight and sensitivity will enable a senior executive to motivate employees in a way that will establish him or her as an extraordinary leader.

Leaders who cannot (or will not) empathize with the needs of their employees will fail because they will not be able to influence others to do what is necessary for business success. The foundation of successful leadership in business today is the ability of senior executives to empathize with a diverse group of employees, customers, and competitors by understanding the varying influences in their lives.

This is easier said than done because, in many ways, developing the skill of empathy is like learning to read. You will never be able to learn to read if you don't practice with very basic books and progress to more complicated books gradually. Likewise, you will never learn to empathize and lead others effectively if you do not gradually develop deeper and deeper sensitivity to the unique influences in the lives of people who are very different than you are. It is important to note that learning to empathize with others requires both practice and self-reflection. You cannot develop the ability to empathize with others if you are not skilled at understanding the influences in society and in your life.

Most people are not aware that it is virtually impossible to effectively understand the influences in other people's lives if they do not understand key influences in their own life. For example, many people ignore the fact that their political views are based on the positive or negative influences of their parents. They identify with conservatives, moderates, or liberals primarily because they either adopted or rebelled against their parents' political beliefs. However, far too often, these same people mistakenly assume that their political preference is based purely on a critical analysis of party platforms. Consequently, these individuals have great difficulty understanding why someone would join a different political party. If they had taken time to understand (and accept) the power of influence on their personality and political preferences, they would be better able to empathize with the perspective of a person who was likely influenced by circumstances beyond his or her control to join a different party.

The concept of *Influence Awareness* is an essential component of individual and organizational leadership in the business world because it provides a framework through which anyone can develop the very difficult skill of empathy. I have discovered that, before some people can effectively explore influences in their personal life, they need to be convinced of the impact of influence in society. The best way to convince people of this is to explore the writings of an author who has provided valuable insight on the important role influence plays in the world.

No recent writer has done more to help the world understand the power of influence than Malcolm Gladwell. His *New York Times* #1 best-selling books *The Tipping Point, Blink,* and *Outliers* transformed the way that people viewed influence in their lives. These books have changed parenting, coaching, and everyday living for millions of people around the world. I developed and trademarked the *Intelligent Influence* process before I read his excellent books; however, after reading his books, I realized that *Intelligent Influence: The 4 Steps of Highly Successful Leaders and Organizations* provides the framework for implementing much of what readers have learned from Gladwell's extraordinary insights.

The latest edition of *The Tipping Point* begins with a section called "Acclaim for Malcolm Gladwell's *The Tipping Point*." The very first quote in this section comes from the well-respected writer Deidre Donahue of *USA Today*. She is quoted as saying: "One of the most interesting aspects of Gladwell's book is the way it reaffirms that human beings are profoundly social beings influenced by and influencing other human beings, no matter how much technology we introduce into our lives."

This extremely insightful statement is the reason why the concept of *Intelligent Influence* has the potential, over time, to reach a "tipping point" that will change the way that people around the world run their businesses and live their lives. Influence is not only the foundation of business success, it is the primary reason that we all *do what we do and think the way we think*. The strategic management of influence in our lives is the foundation of both happiness and the attainment of personal and organizational goals.

It is only fitting to begin this chapter by examining the influences in Malcolm Gladwell's life and the relationship between his extraordinary research and the *Intelligent Influence Framework*. Malcolm Gladwell was born in Fareham, Hampshire, England, on September 3, 1963. His mother Joyce was a black psychotherapist born in Jamaica and his father Graham Gladwell was a white mathematics professor born in England. He spent the first five years of his life in England and moved to Elmira, Ontario, Canada, when he was six. Gladwell's interest in research and writing was influenced by the time he spent with his father at work in his office at the University of Waterloo and his mother's passion for writing.

He graduated from the University of Toronto's Trinity College in 1984, and covered business and science for *The Washington Post* from 1987 to 1996. That year, he joined *The New Yorker* and focused on exploring academic research for insight and inspiration. He has indicated on numerous occasions that he was not an extraordinary college student. However, after graduation, he developed a deep passion for seamlessly integrating academic research and well-written prose.

As I will prove through the case studies in this book, the amazing power of *Intelligent Influence* comes from the very first step in the process of strategically using influence. This step, which I call *Influence Awareness*, enables individuals and organizations to understand their past in a way that provides the insight, confidence, and energy needed to achieve extraordinary future goals. For example, Gladwell's understanding and acceptance of the unique influence of each of his parents served as the foundation of his success as a popular researcher and writer.

He gained great notoriety from an article published in the *New Yorker* on June 3, 1996, called "The Tipping Point." That well-liked piece was followed by another popular article called "The Coolhunt" which was published in the *New Yorker* on March 17, 1997. These two articles were the foundation of his first book *The Tipping Point* for which he received a $1-million advance. More than 5 million people have purchased his books, making him one of the most popular authors of the last decade.

What is it that has made these books so appealing? Why have the books changed the way that people view themselves and the world? The answer to these questions lies in the concept of *Influence Awareness*. Gladwell's books are unique because they provide surprising insight into the way that people and organizations are influenced. He is one of the first authors to provide comprehensive research-based evidence proving that influence is the primary reason why people do what they do.

The Tipping Point describes the particular moment when an idea, trend, or social behavior has sufficient influence to spread like wildfire. His second book *Blink* explains the role of influence in a person's ability to make educated split-second decisions. His third book *Outliers* documents the role of influence in the success or failure of people and organizations. These well-written books provide valuable *Influence Awareness* information for readers.

Influence Awareness

I created *Intelligent Influence* to help people manage the influences in their lives and enhance the way that they interact with one another. I designed the *Intelligent Influence Framework* to visually depict the four steps of the *Intelligent Influence* process. The first step is *Influence Awareness* which is shown in the first box below:

Intelligent Influence Framework™

	Internal Influence	*External Influence*
Influence Understanding	*Step 1* **Influence Awareness**	*Step 2* **Influence Impact**
Influence Actions	*Step 3* **Influence Management**	*Step 4* **Influence Maximization**

As explained in the introduction, each of the four boxes depicts both a step in the *Intelligent Influence* process and an *Influence Competence*. Each of these competencies is a learned capacity, based on *Intelligent Influence*, that results in outstanding performance in any endeavor that requires significant human interaction. Anyone, who is able to effectively utilize each of the four steps and competencies effectively, can be considered to be using *Intelligent Influence*.

I have learned (through my research of hundreds of businesses and my extensive management consulting experience) that every organization and individual who has achieved extraordinary success has consciously or unconsciously utilized each of these four steps/competencies. Throughout *Intelligent Influence: The 4 Steps of Highly Successful Leaders and Organizations*, I will use case studies to demonstrate how the four competencies in the *Intelligent Influence Framework* are the secret to individual and organizational success.

Each of the subsequent chapters in this book support the guiding premise that the business leaders who understand how to implement these steps will be extraordinarily successful. These enlightened individuals have a better sense of their strengths and weaknesses and those of the organization they lead. They have specific strategies for improving themselves and their companies, even in the most challenging economic times. They inspire employees and connect with consumers in a way that consistently increases productivity and profitability.

This framework is initiated through exercises designed to create *Influence Awareness* in an individual or organization. This first step of the *Intelligent Influence* process refers to the conscious effort by individuals or organizations to understand how they have been influenced. I define *Influence Awareness* for an individual as *"the process of understanding the most significant ways in which a person has been influenced in the past and how that person is currently influenced."* Likewise, *Influence Awareness* for an organization is *"the process of understanding the most significant ways in which an organization has been influenced in the past and how the organization is currently influenced."*

Knowing the past is in many ways the secret of creating an extraordinary future. It is essential that individuals and organizations take an inventory of both the ways that they have been influenced and the manner in which they influence others. Every executive has been influenced by family members, classmates, co-workers, previous experiences, what they have read, and popular entertainment to *do what they do and think the way they think.*

Every company has been influenced by its history, corporate culture, other corporations, customers, government, and the financial markets to operate business in a certain way. By assessing how prior influences impact what they do and how they think, individuals and organizations can identify the areas of improvement that they need to achieve their objectives.

The myth of the self-made man or woman is just that—a "myth." We are all products of the influences in our lives. No one in history has become successful without significant help from one or more influential people. Whether we choose to admit it or not, each of us has been influenced in many different ways by many different people on many different subjects. It is essential that we come to terms with those influences and understand the way they impact how and what we do today.

Most of us can identify more than one teacher who was a positive influence in our lives when we were in school. We remember the English teacher who inspired us to read (or write) or the math teacher that made algebra fun. We remember the history teacher that made the past come alive or the science teacher that created interesting educational experiments.

Many of us occasionally think about the adults who taught us right from wrong and influenced us to follow the career path we are on today. We recall the boss who inspired us to succeed and the co-workers that made our job fun. We reminisce about the amazing team that we worked with on a successful project, about the fantastic promotion and raise that we got because we had a boss who recognized our value to the organization.

Each of these individuals influenced us to be the people we are today. However, surprisingly, most of us spend little time reflecting on the extensive influence that they had on our lives. These people did not know it at the time; but each of them utilized some of the concepts of *Intelligent Influence,* in one way or another, to motivate and inspire us to succeed.

It is important to note that every human being on earth has also been impacted by bad influences. The negative people (or experiences) behind these influences play a significant role in influencing how we live our life today. It is, therefore, equally important (even though it is sometimes painful) to reflect on the role of negative influences in our personal development.

What influences have shaped who you are today? What influences have contributed to making your organization what it is today? The process of putting the *Intelligent Influence Framework* into action requires, first and foremost, a comprehensive *awareness* of influences, past and present, in your career, in your business, and in the market overall.

We do what we do, think the way we think, and like what we like largely because of significant influences in our lives. The same is true for organizations. They sell what they sell and operate the way they operate, in a large part, due to both internal and external influences. It is important to note that *Influence Awareness* is a skill that can be enhanced by developing the important habit of regularly reflecting on the people and situations that have had the greatest influence on your life and the life of the organization you lead. One of my favorite examples of a company that effectively utilized *Influence Awareness* as the foundation of their extraordinary success comes from the Clairol Company.

Influence Awareness at Clairol

The Clairol Company was founded in 1931 by enterprising chemist Lawrence Gelb and his wife Joan (who had a passion for anything related to hair care). It is believed that they named the company "Clairol" after a hair-coloring product that they discovered while traveling through France. The Clairol Company was initially focused on selling hair-coloring products directly to beauty salons. However, in 1949, everything changed when they developed the "Miss Clairol Hair Color Bath." This revolutionary new product became an instant hit because it was the most innovative way ever invented for women to color their hair. Their one-step, hair-coloring product, introduced to salons in 1950, significantly increased the demand for the product and the influence of the company in the hair care industry.

As soon as the Hair Color Bath was invented, Lawrence Gelb and the company's other senior executives knew intuitively that they had to initiate the *Influence Awareness* process to determine how they could maximize their influence on women consumers in a manner that would lead to extraordinary sales. They began by examining both their corporate culture (*Internal Influence*) and corporate branding (*External Influence*). Prior to the introduction of this exciting new product, Clairol, like most small companies, had an entrepreneurial culture focused on selling directly to as many beauty salons as possible. Most of their income came from sales driven by the close relationships between sales people and their customers. Very little income came from sales driven by the company's brand.

However, they knew that the creation of an industry-changing product would force them to rely less on sales relationships and more on the branding of the company. This *Influence Awareness* assessment convinced the leadership of the company to transform the culture of the company from one that was sales-force-driven to one that was brand-driven. Instead of simply attempting to make the company a very profitable enterprise, employees were inspired to focus on the potential for the company to be the global brand leader in the hair care industry.

Leaders of successful companies recognize that they must initiate the *Influence Awareness* process every time they are considering strategic business changes. The development of Miss Clairol Hair Color Bath for the home, combined with the realignment of the culture and corporate focus, led the company to undertake the *Influence Awareness* process once again. They recognized that they could not on their own develop the brand awareness that they needed to develop a successful global product. This analysis made them aware that they needed to hire an advertising company that would help them establish the powerful brand identity necessary to maximize their influence with women consumers around the world.

Consequently, in 1955, they hired the advertising firm Foote, Cone & Belding to develop an impactful campaign that significantly increased product sales. The advertising campaign was led by Shirley Polykoff. Shirley, a legendary female advertising executive and the only woman in this role in the agency, was the perfect person for this project. She took the company through yet another *Influence Awareness* review process and explained that their branding strategy had to be based on the fact that women were very private about their hair care. Most women, at the time, did not want their friends or even family members to know whether or not they colored their hair.

Like many of the best advertising executives in history, Shirley instinctively knew that the only way for the campaign to be extraordinarily successful was to design it in a way that would be extremely sensitive to the influences of the female consumers they were targeting. Her extraordinary *Influence Awareness* enabled her to develop a legendary slogan that has changed the hair coloring industry. Like so many other iconic advertising slogans, the famous phrase that she came up with grew out of a real life experience. It is believed that when Shirley's future mother-in-law first met her, she discreetly asked her then-boyfriend if Shirley colored her hair. To market the "Miss Clairol Hair Color Bath," this unfortunate interaction inspired her to develop the phrase: "Does she . . . or doesn't she?" She felt that this phrase would influence women to buy the product because it appealed to their desire for both beauty and discretion.

The idea for the campaign was not an instant hit inside the advertising agency and with some organizations. Shirley initially had a difficult time convincing the agency to use the campaign because many of the men thought the question was too racy to be effective with women. They lacked the *Influence Awareness* necessary to see the extraordinary value of this slogan. She eventually convinced the agency to use the campaign. However, some companies were reluctant to run the advertisements because the male executives were afraid that there would be a "sleazy" interpretation of the phrase.

For example, *Life Magazine* was reluctant to run the ad campaign because the male executives thought it was too racy. Shirley's response is right out of the *Intelligent Influence* playbook. She recognized that these executives lacked the *Influence Awareness* necessary to understand the market for this product and suggested that the *Life Magazine* executives (all of whom were male) poll the women in the office to see what they thought of the ads. As expected, the women loved the advertising. Shirley knew that women would identify with the campaign because she understood how women think and are influenced. She recognized that the phrase is only sexually suggestive to those people whose minds are already in the "gutter." She knew that a racy connotation to this phrase would never enter the mind of the average wholesome woman. However, it is interesting to note that the negative connotations of the phrase obviously entered the mind of her male co-workers and some of the male senior executives in corporations who were worried about running the ads.

This campaign became one of the most successful in history because it was built on solid *Influence Awareness* and convinced millions of consumers around the world to buy Clairol products. Prior to this campaign, coloring women's hair was considered a deceitful and sleazy activity by many women. However, this amazing advertising campaign built on *Influence Awareness* completely changed the mindset of most women consumers. By 1962, more than 70% of women in the United States colored their hair. Clairol dominated this market and increased revenues by more than

400% in the first six years of the campaign. Clairol was purchased by Bristol Myers Squibb (BMS) in 1959 from Lawrence Gelb and his family.

Even today, Clairol, which was purchased by Proctor & Gamble in 2001 from BMS, dominates the hair coloring market. Lawrence's Gelb's sons Richard and Bruce were influenced to carry on his legacy of *Intelligent Influence*. Richard became a legendary BMS executive serving as CEO of BMS from 1972 to 1993. Bruce also served as a BMS executive but became best known as the ambassador to Belgium under President George H.W. Bush. As readers will learn throughout this book, the foundation of every successful company is the successful implementation of *Influence Awareness* in the early stages of strategic planning and product development.

The Influence Awareness Process

As described earlier, *Influence Awareness* for an individual is defined as "*the process of understanding the most significant ways in which a person has been influenced in the past and how that person is currently influenced.*" Likewise, *Influence Awareness* for an organization is defined as the "*the process of understanding the most significant ways in which an organization or target market has been influenced in the past and how the organization or target market is currently influenced.*" There are five fundamental questions that every individual and organization should ask to complete the process of *Influence Awareness*. These are the following:

> *1) What have been the major influences in my life, the customers I am selling to, or the life of the company I lead?*
>
> This is an important question that motivates people to begin to reflect on the influences that have made them think the way they think and do what they do.
>
> *2) How have these influences impacted what I do and/or how my company operates?*
>
> This question motivates people to reflect on the reasons why they do what they do. The answers to this question provide insight into a person (or a company's) strengths and developmental needs.

3) What are the key influences in the lives of the people I interact with on a regular basis (family, friends, co-workers, etc.) and how do these influences affect their actions?

This question helps people understand the reasons why other people think the way they think and do what they do. It provides valuable insight into the strategies a person must use to increase the positive influence that one has on others.

4) What are the key influences in the lives of my customers and how do these influences affect their buying habits?

The answers to this question provide the key to influencing customers in a manner that enables a company to significantly increase sales.

5) Do I spend enough time with people who have been influenced very differently than I have?

Extraordinarily successful people spend considerable time with people who have been influenced very differently. This helps them develop a deeper understanding of ways to effectively influence a broader group of people. In addition, spending time with people who have different perspectives is one of the secrets of developing innovative new ideas.

The individuals and organizational leaders that regularly ask these *Influence Awareness* questions will be more sensitive to the ways in which they have been influenced and the influence-based needs of others. They will, therefore, be in a better position to effectively utilize the *Intelligent Influence* process to achieve extraordinary success. This first step in the process provides the foundation needed to complete the second step which I call *Influence Impact* and describe in detail in the next chapter.

CHAPTER 2

Influence Impact:
Mrs. G TV and Appliances

Amazing Influence Patterns

Every extraordinary business executive and corporation has a solid understanding of the influence that they have on their co-workers and customers respectively. Successful senior executives know (consciously or subconsciously) what they must do to have the most positive and sustainable influence on the different people that work for them. They understand that they may have to be more authoritative in directing Jane on a project and more inspirational in motivating Ted to do the same job. In very much the same way, highly profitable corporations know how to influence their target customers to buy their products. They recognize that some of their most loyal customers stay with the brand because it is innovative while others buy the company's goods or services because of the organization's outstanding reputation.

The best management consultants help senior executives develop comprehensive strategies focused on increasing productivity and profitability. They provide corporate leaders with a valuable outside perspective, information about best practices in other industries, and utilize their exceptional analytical skills to solve complex business problems. This priceless combination of attributes frequently helps clients generate tens of millions of dollars in increased revenue. I was blessed to start my business career as a management consultant and, while I was still in my 20s, learned the best practices of some of the most successful leaders in business.

Over my 25 years in the management consulting profession, I have had a chance to advise and observe corporations in many of the major industries. In addition, I have consulted to many government agencies and nonprofit organizations. These amazing experiences have helped me develop a passion for reading business case studies and biographies of some of the most successful people and organizations in history. Several years ago, as I was researching the role of influence on individual and organizational success, I noticed an interesting pattern related to the relationship between success and influence. The foundation of the success of corporations and individuals was the manner in which they utilized six very distinct types of influences.

These six specific types of influence have often been overlooked because they have been buried in the broad concept of leadership. Unfortunately, the word "leadership" has become the catch-all phrase for everything that is good or bad in the business world. Far too many people have attempted to over-simplify the formula for business success. They believe that having a great CEO is the one and only reason that companies become industry leaders. These same people are also convinced that poor CEO leadership is the only reason companies fail. CEO leadership is clearly extremely important to the profitability of a company. However, success or failure of a company is never the result of just one man or one woman. Success is based on the strategic use of influence of a company's entire leadership team. Many very smart people mistakenly believe that the solution to any company's woes is simply to hire or promote natural-born leaders. They do not understand that people can learn to be great leaders and that the effective use of the six types of *Intelligent Influence* by a CEO and his or her leadership team are the "DNA" of corporate leadership success. The positive types of influence described below are the foundation of the intelligent use of influence in business.

Authority Influence

There are many insightful experts on leadership who have done a masterful job of describing great leadership. These individuals have written some amazing books on leadership that hint at the seamless connection between successful individual and organizational leadership and influence.

Unfortunately, there is very little written about the six different types of influence that form the foundation of successful leadership.

The more I studied the success or failure of organizations and individuals, the clearer it became that their success was connected to the specific type (or combination of types) of influence that they had on co-workers, customers, and/or the general public. The first and most obvious type of individual or organizational influence relates to the influence that an individual or organization has due to a person's position in an organization or a company's position in an industry.

The CEOs of Fortune 500 companies have a certain amount of inherent authority simply because of their title. Coca-Cola's dominant position as the leading soft drink company obviously has given it tremendous authority in the beverage industry. Dictionary.com defines the word *authority* as "*the power to determine, adjudicate, or otherwise settle issues or disputes; jurisdiction; the right to control, command, or determine.*" I, therefore, call the influence based on position, authority, or ability to command *Authority Influence*^{TM}. Every organization has leaders who have this type of influence because of their position or job title. However, the best leaders understand that possessing this type of influence is not enough. They instinctively attempt to develop one or more of the five other types of influence to increase their impact in the organization.

Belief Influence

Many people thought that Jeff Bezos was crazy when he quit his lucrative job on Wall Street to move to the State of Washington to start an online bookstore, named "Amazon.com," in the early days of internet commerce. Bezos has become one of the most successful internet entrepreneurs in history because of his ability to first influence investors, then co-workers, and eventually consumers to believe that purchasing books and other products over the internet was the retail marketplace of the future.

In the early days of Amazon.com (when it was not profitable), he had to convince people that Amazon would eventually become a successful business. He did this by influencing them to believe in something that was not immediately susceptible to rigorous proof. He had to convince people to have faith in the belief that an internet retailer can be a profitable large business. Dictionary.com defines the word *belief* as "*confidence in the truth or existence of something not immediately susceptible to rigorous proof.*" I, therefore, call the type of influence derived by convincing people of something that is not immediately susceptible to rigorous proof *Belief Influence*[TM]. The *Belief Influence* of Jeff Bezos has not only been the foundation of his internet retail success, it has changed the way the world views the internet.

Inspiration Influence

It is one thing to influence people to believe in something that does not yet exist. However, it is an entirely different thing to influence people to develop a passion for a person, an organization, or a product. Richard Branson is one of the exceptional business leaders who has influenced employees, customers, and the general public to develop a passion for multiple products and new businesses (usually bearing his signature brand name "Virgin"). Branson understood the power of music to connect emotionally with consumers. He began Virgin Records in 1972 and started the label with the hit record *Tubular Bells* by Mike Oldfield (which stayed on the UK music charts for an amazing 247 weeks). He convinced millions of consumers to develop a passion for Virgin records by using his initial success to sign legendary artists with a passionate following like The Rolling Stones, The Sex Pistols, and Genesis.

Branson has influenced consumers to develop an emotional connection to new products and services by parlaying his success in the record business into success with Virgin Airlines, Virgin Mobile, and hundreds of other businesses. He has expanded his personal brand and the passionate following of his fans by attempting to set world daredevil records by boat and hot air balloon. Dictionary.com defines the word *inspiration* as "*to fill or affect with a specified feeling.*" I, therefore, call the type of influence derived from the ability to motivate people to feel an intense passion that compels them to act in a particular way *Inspiration Influence*[TM].

People often confuse *Belief Influence* with *Inspiration Influence* because both generate a following of one type or another. Many extraordinary leaders demonstrate both types of influence. However, in distinguishing between these two types of influence, it is important to understand that you can convince someone to believe (or have faith) in something unproven, even though they don't have a passion for it. However, *Inspiration Influence* comes from influencing people to have a passion for or strong emotional connection with a leader, the organization he or she leads, or the products being promoted. Jeff Bezos has been the type of leader who has influenced employees to believe more in the power of internet retail than in his personal brand. Richard Branson, on the other hand, has been the type of inspirational leader who has influenced employees to develop a passion for him and his personal brand. This type of influence has enabled him to start hundreds of very different and unrelated businesses. Clearly, Richard Branson's *Inspiration Influence* has been one of the major secrets of his success in business.

Reputation Influence

It is often assumed that *Authority Influence* is the only type of influence that matters. However, in researching influential individuals and companies, it became clear that many CEOs and industry leaders suffered because they did not possess other equally important types of influence. The rapid demise of companies (and their CEOs) with tremendous *Authority Influence* like Arthur Anderson, Lehman Brothers, Enron, and Lucent indicated that this type of influence in and of itself was not sufficient for long-term success.

One of the major reasons for the downfall of these companies was the tremendous damage to their reputation that was caused by their poor business practices. The negative influence of their bad reputation clearly hurt their position as one of the leading authorities in their respective industries. In contrast, the reputation of a company like Johnson & Johnson, after CEO James Burke masterfully handled the Tylenol crisis, was enhanced in a way that led to increased profitability. Clearly, a company's or individual's reputation plays a vital role in the amount of influence that they have in a position or industry. Dictionary.com defines the word *reputation* as *"the estimation in which a person or thing is held."* I, therefore, call the type of influence derived from the broad-based respect of others *Reputation Influence^{TM}*.

Resource Influence

There is clearly an inherent competitive advantage held by companies that have access to tremendous financial resources. Fortune 500 companies have used their resource-based influence to buy smaller companies that will help them eliminate new competitors and/or expand their penetration in the marketplace. For example, Google's use of its tremendous financial and stock resources to acquire YouTube for $1.65 billion in cash and stock, in 2006, has helped it expand its brand well beyond internet word searches. This strategic purchase enabled Google to corner the search market by dominating the internet word search and internet video search markets.

In much the same way as corporations, senior executives (who control the access to financial, technology, human, or other resources) wield tremendous influence in an organization. Dictionary.com defines the word *resource* as "*a source of supply, support, or aid, especially one that can be readily drawn upon when needed.*" I, therefore, call the type of influence based on the ability to control and share valuable personal or corporate assets *Resource Influence*^{TM}.

Thought Influence

The late Apple CEO Steve Jobs is one of the most admired CEOs in history because of his success in remaining an exceptional thought leader in a large corporation. His extraordinary ability to lead the development of immensely popular innovative technology products, that consumers were not aware that they needed, is legendary. Jobs knew long before they were developed that the iPod, iPhone, and iPad would change the way that millions of people lived their lives. He was one of those rare business leaders who influenced the world because of his ability to think, reason, and imagine. Dictionary.com defines the word *thought* as "*the capacity or faculty of thinking, reasoning, imagining.*" I, therefore, call the type of influence derived from a person's or organization's innovative thinking, reasoning, and imagining *Thought Influence*^{TM}.

When presenting the six types of *Intelligent Influence*, I am often asked about the role of fear, intimidation, anger, and other negative influences in the business world. Clearly, there are more than six types of influence in business and life. However, the six described above, as we will see in our case studies, are the only ones that are the foundation of the sustainable positive influence that is at the heart of *Intelligent Influence*. The problem with negative influences is that they fail to achieve long-term results because they are not sustainable. In business, people eventually get tired of leaders using negative influence and either rebel or leave the company. However, the intelligent use of influence is sustainable because it inspires people to do what leaders want them to do because they genuinely want to do it.

Influence Impact

As we discussed in the previous chapter, the first step in the process of developing *Intelligent Influence* is *Influence Awareness*. The second step is to understand how a person, project team, or organization currently influences others in each of the six types of *Intelligent Influence*. I call this *Influence Impact* which is highlighted in the second box in the *Intelligent Influence Framework* diagram below. This important step in the strategic use of influence is defined as "*the process of understanding the most significant ways in which a person, project team, or organization currently influences others and the areas of influence where improvement is needed.*"

Intelligent Influence Framework™

	Internal Influence	*External Influence*
Influence Understanding	*Step 1* ***Influence Awareness***	*Step 2* ***Influence Impact***
Influence Actions	*Step 3* ***Influence Management***	*Step 4* ***Influence Maximization***

One of the most effective tools in the field of human resource management and industrial psychology is an assessment process known as "360-degree feedback." In this type of assessment, feedback about a particular person (or project team) is provided by subordinates, peers, and supervisors. In addition, the person or team being evaluated is asked to complete a self-assessment. This process is different than traditional "performance appraisals" where feedback is provided only by a person's direct supervisor.

The assessments provided by 360-degree feedback provide a very comprehensive perspective on the effectiveness of an employee (or team) in a particular position or project. The results of these assessments provide valuable insight into the training and development needs of an individual or project team. Very often key people in an organization do a fantastic job completing assignments for their boss. However, they are poor managers who force the talented people who work for them to leave the company. In short, they are great at managing up and horrible at managing down. A 360-degree assessment will uncover these types of human interaction problems that will, over time, negatively impact productivity and profitability.

The most effective way to assess your *Influence Impact* on others in the workplace is to complete a 360-degree assessment that measures the extent to which you exhibit each of the six different types of influence. In this assessment, which we call a *360 Influence Assessment^{TM}*, you, your boss, co-workers, and subordinates are given questionnaires designed to gauge their perspective on the amount of influence you have in the organization. There is tremendous value in implementing a *360 Influence Assessment* for every key person in a company. The extent of a person's influence in an organization is the single most important factor in his or her success. An assessment of influence, from multiple perspectives, will help leaders in the organization understand the developmental needs necessary to increase the value that a person (or project team) brings to the organization.

Depending on the scope and breadth of the assessment, this important and complex process requires a great deal of preparation and consulting to administer effectively. However, it is an essential component of high potential employee development. Self-administered and comprehensive *360 Influence Assessments* determine developmental needs by identifying the extent to which a person, project team, or organization utilize the six distinct types of influence. In combination, these types of influence account for the broad spectrum of positive influence of individuals, teams, and organizations in every situation. The brief definitions that we use for each of these types of influence is as follows:

The Six Types of Intelligent Influence

Authority Influence = Influence derived from position or ability to command.

Belief Influence = Influence derived by making people believe in the unknown and/or unproven.

Inspiration Influence = Influence derived from the ability to inspire people to act.

Reputation Influence = Influence derived from the broad-based respect of others.

Resource Influence = Influence derived from sharing valuable assets.

Thought Influence = Influence derived from innovative ideas or skills.

Influence Impact at Mrs. G TV and Appliances

It is a special privilege for me to share the amazing story of one of my favorite strategic planning clients: Mrs. G TV and Appliances. This successful small business, which won the "2012 New Jersey Family Business of the Year Award" and the "2012 Retailer of the Year Award," is one of the leading independent appliance stores in New Jersey. I have enjoyed working with the incredible CEO (and granddaughter of the founder) Debbie Schaeffer. She is doing a phenomenal job of carrying on the family tradition of a customer-friendly, community-focused retail business.

This incredible family enterprise is one of the special independent small businesses that, over the last 75 years, played a vitally important role in helping to make America an economic powerhouse. Large businesses are often given too much credit for the financial success of the United States. Over the last century, it was small independent businesses with annual sales under $15 million, like Mrs. G, that helped to sustain a growing economy by meeting the purchasing needs of average consumers across the country. The high quality service, provided by these independent businesses, helped to make the standard of living in the United States the envy of the world.

Mrs. G was founded by Abe and Beatrice Greenberg in Trenton, New Jersey, under the name of New Jersey Plumbing in 1935. To meet the growing need for household appliances, the company expanded their product line and began selling stoves, refrigerators, washers, and dryers. It became very clear that Beatrice had a real talent and passion for the retail appliance business. She quickly became the face of the company and naturally (like most small business owners) assumed the roles of CEO/ COO/CFO and Head of Sales.

Beatrice was a very tough and savvy businesswoman who treated the people who shopped at her store with genuine love and care. She had a passion for knowing her customers and would extend special credit terms to many consumers who did not have the money to pay for an appliance, in full, at the time of sale. Beatrice became such an icon in the Princeton/Trenton community that the company moved closer to Princeton and changed its name to Mrs. G. It is important to note that this company (like many other Jewish-, women-, and minority-owned small businesses in America at the time) had to face a hidden competitor called "discrimination." The business's name-change took place, at a time and in a geographic area, where some people would not buy products from a Jewish-owned company. Consequently, the company used the name Mrs. G, instead of Mrs. Greenberg, to increase the business's likelihood of success.

The company has overcome every hurdle it has faced so far because of its effective use of *Intelligent Influence*. Mrs. G is one of those special multi-generational, woman-owned businesses that, over the last 77 years, passed ownership from the mother to the daughter to the granddaughter. These dynamic women had never heard of the concept of *Intelligent Influence*. However, like many other successful businesses, Mrs. G has been able to beat the challenges of discriminatory purchasing, local politics, bad economies and big-box stores because of their intuitive use of *Intelligent Influence* in strategic planning.

For many years, Mrs. G did not have any serious competition. Beatrice was a local celebrity and everyone who was anyone in the Princeton to Trenton corridor bought appliances from Mrs. G. However, the opening of big-box stores, within a mile of Mrs. G, seriously threatened the viability of the store. National chain stores like Sears, P.C. Richards, Wal-Mart, Home Depot, and Lowes were aggressively trying to put small competitors out of business by offering appliances and other products priced well below the market. Tragically, many small family businesses around the country could not compete with these big stores and were forced to go out of business.

However, Mrs. G, through the strategic use of *Intelligent Influence*, has been able to beat these big competitors at their own game and succeed in a very challenging marketplace. In the 1980s and 1990s, the big-box stores and other appliance competitors began to cannibalize Mrs. G's sales to her customer base. The biggest threat to the business was the six stores that Home Depot and Lowes opened, in a ten-mile radius, around Mrs. G. These businesses put significant price pressure on the store and forced the family to think strategically about ways that they could maintain the very positive influence that they had on the local customer base. Like any good business leaders, they intuitively followed the steps presented in the *Intelligent Influence Framework*.

Influence Awareness

The Mrs. G's leadership team had never heard of the *Intelligent Influence Framework*; however, they were successful because they made the same business decisions that would naturally flow out of the *Intelligent Influence* process. The first step that they took in developing a strategic plan for the business was *Influence Awareness*. As described in Chapter 2, *Influence Awareness* for a business is defined as "*the process of understanding the most significant ways in which the organization has been influenced in the past and how the organization is currently influenced.*" In developing a strategy to respond to new competitors, the Mrs. G leadership team (which included Tom Gray who is one of the finest, hardest working, and most principled independent store general managers I have ever met) naturally reflected on their history and influence in the community. It became very clear that the biggest historical influence in the company has been their unwavering commitment to being a family business that treats employees and customers as if they were family friends. They, therefore, had to figure out a way to use this historic influence as a competitive advantage.

Influence Impact

The second step in the process was *Influence Impact* where Mrs. G's leadership team gauged the extent of their influence in the current marketplace. They estimated that Mrs. G, in light of the new competition in the marketplace, had lost influence in each of the six types of *Intelligent Influence* in the following ways:

- *Authority Influence* – The company lost some of its *Authority Influence* to the well-known national big-box stores moving into their target market. Through extensive advertising, these companies had cultivated a reputation across the country as the *authorities* in the appliance, hardware, and home repair business. This brilliant positioning caused some consumers in the Princeton to Trenton corridor to question the long-standing authority of Mrs. G.

- *Belief Influence* – Prior to the arrival of this new competition, consumers believed that the products sold by Mrs. G were the best products available at the best price. Many consumers would never think of shopping anywhere else. However, Home Depot and Lowes were able to influence many people to *believe* that their appliances were less expensive and of the same or better quality than those of small stores like Mrs. G.

- *Inspiration Influence* – Instead of being inspired to purchase appliances from a local icon with extraordinary customer service like Mrs. G, consumers were inspired through big-box national advertising and brand recognition to ignore the benefits of personalized service and focus almost exclusively on getting the lowest retail price for their products. Big-box stores successfully *inspired* consumers to develop a passion for buying products from the company with the perceived lowest price and the largest volume of business.

- *Reputation Influence* – In this new consumer era, dominated by advertising claims that bigger is better and cheaper, the *reputation* of single location stores like Mrs. G took a hit. Big-box stores convinced many people that the mom-and-pop stores were outdated and a thing of the past while the new big modern stores represented the future of appliance shopping.

- *Resource Influence* – The subtle message of the big-box advertising was that small stores like Mrs. G did not have the *resources* necessary to give consumers the best appliances at the best price. Many consumers, therefore, stopped shopping at independent stores like Mrs. G.

- *Thought Influence* – The big-box stores also successfully convinced many consumers that they were new and innovative *thought* leaders while the mom-and-pop stores like Mrs. G were stuck in the past with yesterday's thinking.

This *Influence Impact* analysis clearly showed that big-box stores had taken away a great deal of the influence that Mrs. G had on customers in the Princeton/Trenton corridor. Mrs. G still had the advantage of being well-known and active in the local community. They were one of the leading supporters of nonprofit and civic organizations in the Princeton area. They took great pride in offering great service and quality products at discount prices; however, the big-box stores were able to match or beat many of Mrs. G's prices. So, for the first time, Mrs. G did not offer the lowest prices in the area. The store's leadership, therefore, needed to develop a strategy that would allow them to manage their influences in a way that would enable them to regain a competitive advantage over the new financially strong and aggressive big-box competitors.

The *Influence Impact* analysis described above is a critical exercise for every company because it identifies the *Influence Management* steps that need to be taken to regain (or increase) influence in each of the six types of *Intelligent Influence*. We will discuss *Influence Management* in the next chapter. However, as a preview, let's explore the *Influence Management* action steps that Mrs. G took in response to their *Influence Impact* analysis. Their intuitive review of the company's influence was critical in helping the Mrs. G's leadership team recognized that it would be very hard for them to compete with the national big-box stores solely on price.

They, therefore, had to identify a product category and approach in the appliance market that would give them a competitive advantage over the big-box stores. They made a strategic *Intelligent Influence* decision to offer the luxury appliance products that the big-box stores did not specialize in. Mrs. G, therefore, started selling high-end appliances like Miele, Sub-Zero, Thermadore, Viking, and Wolf. This was a perfect business "chess move" because these products required the kind of customer care that only a consumer-focused store like Mrs. G could offer.

Unfortunately, offering high-end products was not enough to regain their position as a local market leader. For the store to thrive, they had to find an *Intelligent Influence* way to compete on price with the big-box stores. If Mrs. G could not compete on price, they would not be able to attract enough customers to the store to reach the sales levels they needed to survive. As a small company, they could only compete on price if they became part of a buying group that purchased the same large volumes of appliances as the big-box stores. Mrs. G, therefore, joined the largest appliance buying and marketing organization in the United States.

The Nationwide Marketing Group is comprised of over 3,000 independent stores with a buying power of more than $12 billion. The alliance of Mrs. G with this group, combined with their strategic focus on high-end products, enabled the company to strategically utilize *Intelligent Influence* in a way that enabled them to successfully compete on both product and price with any appliance store in the area. Their brilliant use of *Influence Impact* analysis enabled them to develop the strategy that helped them regain their leadership position in the appliance market in the Trenton to Princeton corridor. The strategic adjustment in their business approach, as a result of this analysis, increased the influence of Mrs. G in the following ways:

- *Authority Influence* – By offering high-end appliances, Mrs. G regained their position as the *authority* on the nicest and most exclusive products in the industry. This important repositioning re-established them as the market leader for affluent consumers of appliances.

- *Belief Influence* –The ability of Mrs. G to compete with the large stores on price and beat these stores on quality convinced many consumers to *believe* (once again) that Mrs. G was the best local place to go for appliances.

- *Inspiration Influence* – The showroom of the store was transformed in a way that enabled it to showcase high-end appliances. People loved the store design. This beautiful new layout *inspired* customers to reconnect emotionally with the store and its friendly sales team.

- *Reputation Influence* – The resiliency of Mrs. G, at a time when small businesses (because of the influx of big-box stores) were being forced to close, enabled the store to develop a *reputation* as an icon of small independent business. This *reputation* was particularly impressive because this store is one of the few multi-generational small businesses in America that has been passed down from mother to daughter to granddaughter.

- *Resource Influence* – The membership of Mrs. G in the Nationwide Marketing Group gave it the access to the *resources* that it needed to compete on price with large stores.

- *Thought Influence* – The ability of their leadership team to develop innovative new approaches to compete with the large stores established the Mrs. G leadership team as *thought* leaders in the small business world. This helped them gain influence with both customers and other small businesses.

Appliance stores are facing significant business challenges in today's marketplace. This industry has been hurt more than others by the weak global economy. Profit margins have been shrinking and stores are facing growing competition from the internet. The good news is that Mrs. G will continue to thrive as long as they look strategically at ways to increase their *Influence Impact* and make sound business decisions based on this analysis.

Assessing Corporate Influence Impact

The second step in the process of developing *Intelligent Influence* is *Influence Impact*. This important step in the strategic use of influence is defined as "*the process of understanding the most significant ways in which a person, a project team, or an organization currently influences others and the areas of influence where improvement is needed.*" It is important to note that the process of assessing *Influence Impact* for organizations and individuals is different.

Leaders of organizations should assess the *Influence Impact* of their organization by asking the following six key questions (each related to a specific type of influence):

> *1) Does my company have the necessary "authority" to become or remain a market leader in the industry or industries in which we compete?*
>
> This is an important question about the positioning of a company among its competitors. Organizations that are industry leaders have the influence to dictate prices, product design, service approaches, offerings to customers, etc. Companies that are not leaders in their industry generally do not have significant *Authority Influence*. They are, therefore, forced to react to the companies that have this type of influence.

2) Do employees and customers "believe" that the products and/or services that we are offering are better than those of our competitors?

This question helps leaders design a strategy to develop *Belief Influence* by convincing employees and customers to *believe* that the products and/or service offerings of their company are the best available.

3) Are people" inspired" to buy our products and work at the company?

Inspiration Influence is very difficult to cultivate in most corporations because there is very little to positively stimulate human emotions on a regular basis. However, companies in technology, entertainment, and sports depend on this type of influence to motivate people to purchase their products or services. In addition, this type of corporate influence enables companies to recruit talented employees for below market salaries.

4) Is the "reputation" of my company what I would like it to be in the marketplace?

To increase *Reputation Influence* a company must first honestly assess its true *reputation* in the industry. This means formally or informally surveying social media, customers, competitors, employees, vendors, family, and friends. The results of this informal survey are frequently a surprise to company leaders. However, once you have a good sense of the company's true *reputation*, it is essential that a public relations plan be developed to address the areas where the company needs to develop a better *reputation*.

5) Does the company have the "resources" necessary to make the business investments required to maximize its influence on its target market?

Most companies are driven by purely budgetary needs to develop a financial operating plan. They don't think of their financial, human resource, and capital needs in the context of *Resource Influence*. Consequently, they frequently do not have enough *resources* to compete effectively against their biggest competitors. By developing financial plans based on *Resource Influence*, corporations can make the financial investments that will strategically increase the influence that they have on their target market.

6) Has the company established itself as a "thought" leader in its industry?

To increase *Thought Influence*, a company must first create a culture of innovation where new ideas and "out-of-the-box" thinking are not only encouraged, it is rewarded and celebrated. Once this culture is created, the company must fully embrace diversity in every sense of the word (skills, education, experiential, generational, geographic, gender, race, etc.). In the changing business world of today, the companies that have the most *Thought Influence* are those having many smart employees who think very differently because of the diverse influences in their life.

Assessing Individual Influence Impact

Assessing corporate influence is very different than gauging individual influence. A person's *Influence Impact* can typically be assessed by utilizing two types of questions. The first is called an *Influence Frequency Question*^{TM} or IFQ because it relates to the frequency with which certain *Influence Triggers*^{TM} take place. These specific triggers provide great insight into the extent to which a person has a certain type of influence. A sample of the IFQ questions for an individual is provided below:

Influence Frequency Questions (IFQ)

In the space provided, please list the number that corresponds with your perception of the frequency of the activity. Please use the following 1 to 5 scale:

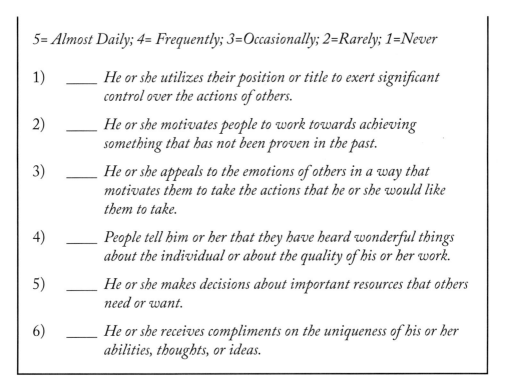

5= Almost Daily; 4= Frequently; 3=Occasionally; 2=Rarely; 1=Never

1) _____ *He or she utilizes their position or title to exert significant control over the actions of others.*

2) _____ *He or she motivates people to work towards achieving something that has not been proven in the past.*

3) _____ *He or she appeals to the emotions of others in a way that motivates them to take the actions that he or she would like them to take.*

4) _____ *People tell him or her that they have heard wonderful things about the individual or about the quality of his or her work.*

5) _____ *He or she makes decisions about important resources that others need or want.*

6) _____ *He or she receives compliments on the uniqueness of his or her abilities, thoughts, or ideas.*

In the business world today, perception is often accepted as reality. How a person is perceived determines the person's success in an organization. Perception is based on influence. People are influenced to perceive a person a certain way. The IFQs are, therefore, extremely important assessment tools because they provide valuable insight into the perceived influence (or lack thereof) of an employee. Far too often, hardworking employees are overlooked because they are perceived not to have the influence necessary to succeed in the organization.

In the example, Question #1 relates to *Authority Influence*. This question is designed to determine if the person is considered by others to have the influence that comes with a powerful position. Question #2 relates to *Belief Influence*. It is focused on identifying if the person is influencing people to believe in a particular project or activity. Question #3 relates to *Inspiration Influence*. This question helps to determine the person's ability to stimulate the emotions of others in a way that makes them more productive.

Question #4 relates to *Reputation Influence*. It helps to gauge if the person has a stellar reputation in his or her organization. Question #5 relates to

Resource Influence. This question sheds light on the extent to which the person controls resources that are valuable to others in the organization. Finally, Question #6 relates to *Thought Influence.* It helps to determine if the person has influence related to innovative ideas, thoughts, or actions. It is amazing how much you learn about a person's influence in an organization when the person, his or her boss, peers, and subordinates complete just 18 of these questions (three on each type of influence).

The second type of self-assessment question, to assess *Influence Impact,* relates explicitly to the type of influence that you and others perceive that you are using on a regular basis. We call these *Intelligent Influence Quotient*^{TM} questions or IIQs because they relate to the extent of a person's *Intelligent Influence* in the organization. In the self-administered assessment, we ask people to answer the questions below as honestly as possible from their perspective as well as that of their boss, co-workers, and subordinates. In the standard *360 Influence Asessment,* we interview the employee as well as his or her boss, key co-workers, and subordinates to determine how they rate the IIQ of the employee in each of the six types of *Intelligent Influence.*

The Six Types of Intelligent Influence

Authority Influence = Influence derived from position or ability to command.

Belief Influence = Influence derived by making people believe in the unknown and/or unproven.

Inspiration Influence = Influence derived from the ability to inspire people to act.

Reputation Influence = Influence derived from the broad-based respect of others.

Resource Influence = Influence derived from sharing valuable assets.

Thought Influence = Influence derived from innovative ideas or skills.

Intelligent Influence Quotient (IIQ)

On a scale of 1-10 (10 being "very high"; 1 being "very low"), how do you think your boss, co-workers, and subordinates (answer the questions three different times to record your answers from the perspective of your boss, co-workers, and subordinates) would rate you on the following types of influence?

_____ Authority Influence: Influence based on position, authority or ability to command.

_____ Belief Influence: Influence derived by making people believe in the unknown and/or unproven.

_____ Inspiration Influence: Influence derived from the ability to stimulate the emotions of others.

_____ Reputation Influence: Influence derived from the broad-based respect of others.

_____ Resource Influence: Influence based on the ability to share valuable personal assets.

_____ Thought Influence: Influence derived from someone's innovative ideas or skills.

Senior executives should conduct this type of influence self-assessment, not only from their boss's perspective, but also from the perspective of their key co-workers and the people that report to them. The individuals and organizational leaders who regularly ask the *Influence Impact* questions, outlined in this chapter, have a better sense of their *Influence Developmental Needs*[TM] and those of the corporation that they lead. They will, therefore, be in a better position to effectively utilize the *Influence Management* process to achieve extraordinary success. We describe this important process in detail in the next chapter.

CHAPTER 3

Influence Management:
Amazon

Unconscious Competence

The sport of tennis has been a very important part of my life since I was a little child. Over the years, I have been able to earn a United States Tennis Association (USTA) sectional or national ranking in singles in the 18-and-Under, Men's Open 25-, 30-, 35-, and 40-age groups. In addition, at 50, I had the good fortune of winning the gold medal in tennis in Men's Singles in the New Jersey Senior Olympics. My research on influence uncovered a fascinating insight. Amazingly, the *Intelligent Influence* development of successful executives and corporations mirrors the development of ranked tennis players.

When I first hit a tennis ball with my father at five years old, I was at a stage that I call "unconscious incompetence." I knew very little about the sport of tennis and had no idea how bad I was. When I started to take tennis lessons from my dad (and in a free urban community tennis program called Sportsman's Tennis Club in Boston), I learned how bad I was and achieved a state that I call "conscious incompetence." As I got better, I learned how to get the racquet back, turn my body, adjust my feet properly, hit the ball in front of me, and follow through. This enabled me to enter the state that I call "conscious competence." In short, I knew how to play when I was mentally focused on the game. However,

I reached the final stage of tennis development when I won my very first tournament at age 14 in Baltimore, Maryland, for an American Tennis Association (ATA) Baltimore Tennis Championship. In this tournament, I demonstrated that I had reached the state of "unconscious competence" where I had enough control of my tennis game to focus on beating my opponents instead of thinking about hitting the ball properly.

The process of developing the skill of *Intelligent Influence* is very similar to the process of learning to play tennis well. When most people (or organizations) begin the process of *Influence Awareness*, they are in a state of *Unconscious Influence Incompetence*^{TM}. They are not aware of the ways in which they have been influenced to think they way they think and do what they do. When they begin the process of *Influence Impact*, they are entering the state of *Conscious Influence Incompetence*^{TM} where they are beginning to recognize their *Influence Weaknesses*^{TM}. This important insight helps them to understand the ways in which they must manage the influences in their life to be more successful. This leads them to the process of *Influence Management* where they are in a state of *Conscious Influence Competence*^{TM}. They know what they have to do to strategically utilize influence to achieve specific goals. The final step in the process is *Influence Maximization* where individuals or organizations demonstrate *Unconscious Influence Competence*^{TM} by being able to instinctively utilize *Intelligent Influence* to attain extraordinary success.

Influence Management

This chapter describes the third step in the *Intelligent Influence* process which I call *Influence Management* (see Step 3 in the *Intelligent Influence Framework* diagram that follows). In this step, which can be described as *Conscious Influence Competence*, individuals and organizations are strategically bringing the influences into their life necessary to achieve specific goals. *Influence Management* is defined as *"the intentional effort by a person, group, or organization to utilize a developmental plan designed to strategically increase one's External Influence."*

Intelligent Influence Framework™

	Internal Influence	External Influence
Influence Understanding	Step 1 **Influence Awareness**	Step 2 **Influence Impact**
Influence Actions	Step 3 **Influence Management**	Step 4 **Influence Maximization**

Listed below are the two simple *Influence Management* equations that depict the relationship between the variables in this process. The first equation below applies to individuals:

Individual Influence Management™

Personality Type (P) + Skills (S) + Internal Influence (I) = External Influence (E)

Where the symbols represent the following:

P = The personality type of an individual.

S = The skills and abilities a person possesses.

I = The developmental influence action (training, coaching, team building, etc.).

E = The ways in which this person influences others as a result of the person's actions.

The equation is very similar for organizations. However, the nomenclature is different. Instead of "personality," organizations have a "culture." Instead of "skills," organizations have "capabilities." The second equation below applies to organizations:

Organization Influence Management [TM]

Organization Culture (O) + Capabilities (C) + Internal Influence (I) = External Influence (E)

Where the symbols represent the following:

O = The organization's culture.

C = The capabilities of the organization (research, development, production, sales, etc.).

I = The developmental influence action (training, consulting, acquisitions, divestitures, selling "loss-leader" products, etc.).

E = The ways in which the organization influences others as a result of the organization's actions.

These two equations highlight the important relationship between personality/culture, skills/capabilities, and *Internal Influence* in determining the *External Influence* needed for success. Executives with the personality type and skills necessary to become a CEO often never receive the *Internal Influence* they need to attain that goal. Corporations also often fail to strategically use *Internal Influence* to reach their profitability goals, even though they may have an effective corporate culture and strong research, development, production, and sales capabilities.

The most successful individuals keep the end in mind. They focus on specific goals and objectives that can be accomplished by maximizing their influence. They are aware (consciously or subconsciously) of their personality traits and skills, and intentionally manage the ways in which they are influenced (internally) to have the *External Influence* necessary to achieve their goals and objectives.

Famous individuals like U.S. President and Military General Dwight D. Eisenhower, Albert Einstein, Barbara Walters, Christina Aguilera, Warren

Buffet, and Steven Spielberg were successful because they understood how to identify the types of *Internal Influences* that would help them get the most out of their introverted personality and exceptional skills.

The leaders of the most successful organizations also keep the end in mind. They focus on specific goals and objectives that can be accomplished by maximizing the influence of their organization on both employees and customers. They are aware of their organizational culture and capabilities, and intentionally manage the ways in which the employees are influenced so that the organization can have the *External Influence* necessary to achieve their goals and objectives.

Since their founding, the leaders of companies like Coca-Cola, GE, IBM, Microsoft, and WalMart have developed a solid understanding of the culture and capabilities of their respective companies. These leaders provided the *Internal Influence* necessary (through their leadership team, training programs, and the use of outside advisors) to make the most of their corporate cultures and capabilities. This *Internal Influence* blended seamlessly with each of these organization's cultures and capabilities to generate the *External Influence* necessary to place each of these companies among the most successful in history.

Unfortunately, most people ignore the role of influence in their life. Even those individuals most committed to personal development focus on understanding their personality and enhancing their skills while ignoring *Internal Influences*. They, therefore, do not achieve their personal goals and objectives.

Tragically, most organizations ignore the role of *Internal Influence* in the attainment of their goals and objectives. They will focus on improving the technical skills and capabilities of individuals and organizations. However, they do not develop a plan that will seamlessly integrate influence planning with employees' personalities and skills or an organization's culture and capabilities. They, therefore, fail to achieve their financial and operational goals and objectives. *Intelligent Influence* provides a strategic framework for individuals and organizations to increase the probability of success in targeted endeavors. As we will see in the case study that follows, Jeff Bezos masterfully utilized the concept of *Influence Management* to make Amazon one of the most powerful companies in the world.

Influence Management at Amazon

Jeffrey Preston Jorgensen was born in Albuquerque, New Mexico, on January 12, 1964, to 19-year-old Jacklyn Gise Jorgensen and Ted Jorgensen. Their marriage only lasted a year. Jacklyn later married Cuban immigrant Miguel Bezos when Jeff was five years old. Jeff gained the last name Bezos when he was legally adopted by Miguel who later became an engineer for Exxon in Houston, Texas. He was a young man who loved to read books and was influenced by his engineer dad to develop an interest in science and technology. Jeff's passion for entrepreneurship was fueled by the creation (with his sister) of "The DREAM Institute" when he was in high school to make money over the summer and help students read more books and grow intellectually.

Bezos was an excellent student who graduated from Princeton with a degree in Electrical Engineering and Computer Science in 1985. This technical background provided him with the programming knowledge he would later need to start an e-commerce business that required considerable amounts of complicated software code. However, instead of going to Silicon Valley, Bezos wisely decided to work on Wall Street to develop a better understanding of financial markets. His most significant jobs after Princeton were for Bankers Trust and the hedge fund D.E. Shaw & Co. where he was in charge of examining internet-based investment opportunities.

His decision to found Amazon was influenced by his discovery, as Senior Vice President at D.E. Shaw & Co., that internet usage in the early 1990s was growing at more than 2,000% a year. Bezos had a great job and was doing well on Wall Street; however, he had a deep yearning to create a business that would combine his love for reading, technology, and finance. He, therefore, quit his job; secured a $300,000 investment from his parents; and in the summer of 1994, moved with his wife McKenzie to Bellevue, Washington, to start an internet bookstore. I am sure that most of his friends and family thought he was crazy to leave a job paying him a lot of money to move across the country to start a company selling books on an unproven and relatively new medium called the internet.

Bezos was successful for three main reasons. First, he instinctively had the *Influence Awareness* to understand his influence-driven strengths and weaknesses. Second, he had enough of an intuitive comprehension of

Influence Impact to enable him to recognize that the rapidly growing influence of the internet had the potential to radically change the way books are sold. Finally, his ability to effectively utilize *Influence Management* in the early stages of the company's development was the single most important key to Amazon's amazing success.

As depicted in the *Organization Influence Management* equation, the most successful companies understand their organizational *culture*, their core *capabilities,* and implement the *Internal Influence* they need to achieve the *External Influence* they desire. The *External Influence* that Bezos desired for Amazon was for the organization to be the largest book seller in the world. He created a *culture* of entrepreneurship and hired a team that gave Amazon the *capabilities* of software development, retail sales, and warehouse management.

However, he recognized that the internet at the time was like a big valuable plot of land. The companies that were going to succeed in the long run were those that grabbed as much digital land (internet shoppers) as quickly as possible to be successful. He, therefore, instinctively knew that the *Internal Influence* Amazon needed to achieve the *External Influence* goals was anything that would help it "Get Big Fast!" This became the company's *Influence Management* strategy. The company went online, July 6, 1995; and from that point, Bezos used the mission of urgency to convince investors, employees, customers, and the world that profitability was secondary to growth.

He, therefore, utilized the *Influence Management* concept of selling "loss-leader" books where the company lost money on many of the books sold. However, these lower prices enabled Amazon to steal customers from both local and big-box bookstores. He also focused on acquisitions and investing in the most talented people possible to accelerate the company's growth. These investments were a critical component of the strategy Bezos used to "Get Big Fast." He also invested heavily in software upgrades and business expansion that enabled Amazon to better serve their customers.

He faced growing pressure from investors who were getting very frustrated because the company had rapidly growing sales but was taking longer than most companies to become profitable. Bezos was not an extraordinarily charismatic person; however, he was able to garner *Belief Influence* by convincing investors that his long-term *Influence Management* strategy was sound. The investors were relieved and extremely happy when Bezos took the company public on May 15, 1997, with an opening price of $29.25 which was $11.25 higher than the offering price.

Amazingly, the stock price tripled in its first year as a public company. However, Bezos was still focused on growth into new retail markets (music, software, electronics, apparel, toys, and other products). He, therefore, encouraged people to ignore positive or negative fluctuations in the stock price. Bezos knew that he still had to grow rapidly to maintain his success. Fortunately, his success was being recognized by the world. He was named *Time Magazine* "Man of the Year" in 1999 because of the retail success of Amazon. However, the dot-com "bubble" sent Amazon stock prices to a low of $5.97 a share the following year. Nevertheless, the *Influence Management* focus of Bezos, on growth, paid off.

In the fourth quarter of 2001, Amazon posted its first profit of $5 million or 5 cents a share on sales of $1 billion. It has since grown to sell the same products found in traditional retail stores and is competing directly with legendary companies like Wal-Mart, Macy's, and Sears. In many cases, Amazon is winning the retail war over the icons of the retail industry. Incredibly, in less than 20 years, Jeff Bezos' *Influence Management* strategy of "Get Big Fast!" has enabled Amazon to become one of the most influential retail companies in history.

Corporate Influence Management

As described earlier, the third step in the process of developing *Intelligent Influence* is *Influence Management*. This important step in the strategic use of influence is defined as "*the intentional effort by a person, group, or organization to utilize a developmental plan designed to strategically increase their External Influence.*" I recommend that leaders of organizations assess the *Influence Management* of their organization by asking the following four key questions:

1) What External Influence do I want my company to have over the next three to five years?

This important question forces leaders to determine the strategic direction of the company. It is very hard for a company to effectively complete the *Influence Management* step if it does not have specific *External Influence* goals. For example, Amazon founder Jeff Bezos recognized that the only way that the company would survive in the long run in an internet space, where the barriers to entry are very low, was to "Get Big Fast." Consequently, the first *External Influence* goal of Bezos and his leadership team was to become the best known and largest bookstore in the world by influencing consumers to think of Amazon first when they wanted to buy books. For the company to get the growth that it needed to succeed, it was essential to influence consumers to check book prices on Amazon before they visited anywhere else. Once Amazon became the largest bookseller in the world, they developed subsequent *External Influence* goals focused on becoming the biggest retail store in the world. They did this by influencing consumers to think of buying music, electronics, clothing, shoes, and toys from Amazon before any other retailer.

2) Is the existing "culture" of my organization appropriate to match its long-term business growth strategy (External Influence goals)?

Jeff Bezos instinctively knew that Amazon had to grow quickly so he developed a *culture* of mega-entrepreneurship at Amazon where every employee was focused on rapidly growing the company's share of the retail marketplace. He controlled much of the early hiring and the *culture* to ensure that the Amazon team had the right people with the right attitudes in the right roles.

3) Do my employees have the "skills" necessary to enable the company to achieve its long-term business strategy?

Every extraordinarily successful company understands that it needs to have a mix of employees who, in combination, provide the company with the specific *capabilities* necessary to achieve its targeted business strategy (*External Influence* goals). Bezos knew that he needed employees who were experts in software development, warehouse management, purchasing, and retail management. He, therefore, hired the best people he could find from the best companies he could. This strategy was so successful that Amazon was sued for allegedly hiring executives from Wal-Mart and stealing some of their retail secrets.

4) What Internal Influence does the company need to achieve its External Influence goals?

The best CEOs intuitively understand what type of *Internal Influence* is needed to achieve the company's *External Influence* goals. They are intimately aware of the company's *culture* and *capabilities* and recognize the specific type of *Internal Influence* that is required to achieve *External Influence* goals. The *Internal Influence* that Bezos utilized masterfully was influencing everyone in the organization (through regular communications, training, discussions, workshops, advisors, consultants, etc.) that customer satisfaction was "Job One." Every employee was influenced to provide the quality and customer service necessary to convince consumers to equate buying from Amazon with convenience, low prices, and on-time delivery. Employees were influenced to feel that they were part of a team that was changing the business world in a way that provided value for customers. This motivated employees to work harder together to ensure customer satisfaction. By utilizing this brilliant *Influence Management* strategy, Bezos influenced everyone in the organization to believe that the most important thing that they could help the company do was to "Get Big Fast." The employees responded by making Amazon the fastest growing and most successful internet retail company in history.

Individual Influence Management

Individuals focused on implementing *Influence Management* effectively should ask the following four key questions:

1) What External Influence do I want to have over the next three to five years?

In today's competitive global job market, it is essential that employees consider themselves a free agent in much the same way that athletes do in baseball, basketball, and football. Athletes in these sports pursue very clear *External Influence* goals. Most of the athletes and their sports agents are focused on the *External Influence* of maximizing their income. They choose their team based on the most lucrative financial offer. However, a few elite athletes, like LeBron James in basketball, base the decision on which team to join based on its ability to win a championship. It is essential that you, as an executive with a bright future, decide what your professional goals are in three to five years. This might mean that your *External Influence* goals are becoming the head of your division, a vice president, the CEO, making a certain amount of money, or starting your own business. The most important thing to remember is that it is essential that you have very clear *External Influence* goals (over a defined period of time). If you don't, you are guaranteed to flounder and not have the influence-driven success that you could in your career.

2) What is my" personality type"?

There are a lot of very good personality-type assessments on the market. Some of them, like Myers-Briggs, have been around for many years and offer excellent insight into your *personality* traits. None of these instruments is perfect. However, they do provide valuable information about your strengths and weaknesses. For example, knowing that you are an introvert provides important insight into the type of *Internal Influence* that you need to achieve the *External Influence* goals outlined in your answer to the previous question.

3) What are my "skills"?

I continue to be amazed that very few otherwise intelligent professionals take the time to honestly answer this question. Most professionals assume that they are smart enough to figure anything out so they do not take the time to write down the *skills* that they have and the *skills* that they need to work on. They, therefore, are not able to accurately identify the *Internal Influences* that they need to achieve their *External Influence* goals. If you are a poor public speaker, a weak writer, behind on technical training at your company, or an average team leader, you need to admit your training needs to yourself. These developmental needs are probably obvious to those around you, so you need to admit them to yourself and do something about them immediately.

4) What Internal Influence do I need to achieve my External Influence goals?

Extraordinarily successful professionals understand how to utilize *Influence Management* to succeed at work and spend considerable time thinking about the relationship between their *Internal Influence* needs and their *External Influence* goals. They are intimately aware of their *personality* type and *skills*, and recognize the specific type of *Internal Influence* that is required to achieve their *External Influence* goals. For example, introverts who have an *External Influence* goal of becoming a vice president at their company, but have difficulty managing project teams, should immediately request executive coaching to give them the *Internal Influence* they need to achieve their career goal. The strategic use of *Influence Management* in this way is the secret of career success.

CHAPTER 4

Influence Maximization: Coca-Cola

Influence Maximization

The fourth and most challenging step in the *Intelligent Influence* process is *Influence Maximization* (see Step 4 in the *Intelligent Influence Framework* diagram below). This step is defined as "*the process of maximizing influence with a targeted group of people.*" The ultimate goal in this step is to reach the stage of *Unconscious Influence Competence* where you (or the organization that you lead) instinctively maximizes influence, in every situation, involving significant human interaction.

Intelligent Influence Framework™

	Internal Influence	External Influence
Influence Understanding	Step 1 **Influence Awareness**	Step 2 **Influence Impact**
Influence Actions	Step 3 **Influence Management**	Step 4 **Influence Maximization**

In order to maximize influence, it is essential to understand that the six types of *Intelligent Influence* fall into three very distinct spheres of influence. These spheres are called: The *Behavioral Influence™* sphere; the *Rational Influence™* sphere; and the *Emotional Influence™* sphere and in combination are called the *Caldwell Spheres of Influence™*.

Webster's defines the word *behavior* as "*the manner of conducting oneself.*" The *Behavioral Influence* sphere is defined as "*the ability to influence people to do things and is comprised of Authority Influence and Resource Influence.*" In this sphere of influence, a person or group of people are motivated (because of the position or significant resources of an individual, group, or organization) to follow or ascribe *credibility* to an individual or organization. For example, the #1 and #2 companies, in any major industry, are followed by consumers more than those of any other company in their field. People are, therefore, motivated to do something with these products (buy them, pay attention to their ads, follow their promotions, etc.) because of the *Behavioral Influence* derived from their industry position and access to tremendous resources.

Webster's defines the word *rational* as "*having reason or understanding.*" The *Rational Influence* sphere is defined as "*the ability to influence people to think things and is comprised of Reputation Influence and Thought Influence.*" In this sphere of influence, a person is influenced to think certain things about another person, a group, or an organization because of reputation or innovative ideas. Often people ascribe *creativity* to individuals or organizations that exhibit *Rational Influence.* For example, Albert Einstein's "Theory of Relativity" influenced people to think differently about the universe and the relationship between time and space. His insights helped him develop a reputation as the quintessential genius.

Webster's defines the word e*motion* as "*a state of feeling.*" The *Emotional Influence* sphere is defined as "*the ability to influence people to feel things and is comprised of Belief Influence and Inspiration Influence.*" In this sphere of influence, a person is motivated by an individual, group, or organization to feel certain things because of a certain belief or inspiring words (or actions). Frequently, people ascribe *connection* to individuals exhibiting *Emotional Influence.* For example, Nike's powerful marketing tag line "Just Do It!" connected emotionally in a way that inspired millions of people to both purchase their products and increase the intensity of their workouts.

Jeff Bezos, through his company Amazon, demonstrated *Emotional Influence* by convincing the world to believe in the power of internet retail.

Those individuals or organizations who are able to excel in one or more types of influence in each of these three categories, at the same time, are able to maximize their influence on a specific person or group. The relationship between these categories of influence is depicted by the *Caldwell Spheres of Influence* diagram below:

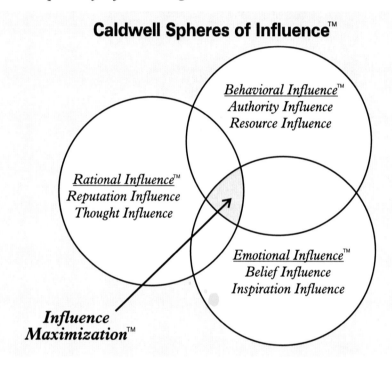

Caldwell Spheres of Influence™

Behavioral Influence™
Authority Influence
Resource Influence

Rational Influence™
Reputation Influence
Thought Influence

Emotional Influence™
Belief Influence
Inspiration Influence

Influence Maximization™

The *Intelligent Influence* process is extraordinarily effective because it helps corporations and leaders move from a state of *Unconscious Influence Incompetence* (*Influence Awareness*) to a state of *Conscious Influence Incompetence* (*Influence Impact*) to a state of *Conscious Influence Competence* (*Influence Management*) and, finally, to the ultimate state of *Unconscious Influence Competence* (*Influence Maximization*). In the state of *Unconscious Influence Incompetence*, corporations or leaders are not aware that their effectiveness is being hindered by their inability to influence others in their workplace.

In the state of *Conscious Influence Incompetence*, corporations or leaders are aware of their influence strengths and weaknesses. In the state of *Conscious Influence Competence*, corporations or leaders are actively attempting to improve their ability to implement *Intelligent Influence* strategies. Finally, in the state of *Unconscious Influence Competence*, corporations or leaders are extraordinarily successful because (without thinking about it) they are utilizing *Intelligent Influence* strategies on a daily basis. This developmental process, which we will explore using Coca-Cola as an example, is the key to success in any activity involving significant human interaction.

Influence Maximization at Coca-Cola

History was about to be made. One of the most influential companies in the world was minutes away from announcing the launch of a new product that many thought would become the best-selling consumer item ever. Millions of people could not wait to hear the future plans of the most iconic business in history. Company executives were equally excited to make this announcement which came on the heels of extensive market research.

These seasoned corporate leaders were convinced that they had conducted sufficient analysis of the consumer marketplace to justify introducing an important new product that would exponentially increase their market share. This announcement, which became a seminal moment in business history, was especially notable because it came less than two months after the death of the legendary CEO who led the company for a record 31 years and refused to allow this type of product introduction.

The announcement of the new product was made in a staged environment that intensified the excitement in the legendary Vivian Beaumont Theatre at New York City's famous Lincoln Center. More than 200 television and newspaper reporters were overjoyed to be the ones covering this major news story about a transformational change in the company's product line. Clearly, the corporation had invested millions of dollars in preparing for this major product introduction which went off, without a flaw, during the announcement. However, on this important day in the company's life, the leaders of the organization had no clue about the "business tsunami" they were about to experience.

80

In spite of their seemingly meticulous planning, this announcement is considered one of the most significant failures in business history. The company was Coca-Cola and the product was "New Coke" which had a new formula. The legendary former CEO was Robert Woodruff who led the company from 1923 to 1954 and refused to allow anyone to consider changing the secret formula of the best-known consumer product in the world.

It is estimated that the change to this incredibly popular soft drink was heard by more than 80% of the United States population in less than 24 hours. Life-long consumers and passionate fans of both Coca-Cola the drink and company were outraged. Millions of people around the world expressed such displeasure with the company's decision the Coca-Cola Company's senior leadership team quickly began developing plans to re-introduce the old product and call it "Coca-Cola Classic."

Within a week of the announcement, the company's 800-number was flooded with thousands of calls a day. Coca-Cola also received more than 40,000 letters complaining about the change. Amazingly, the company lost hundreds of millions of dollars of market share almost instantaneously. The intensity of the consumer rebellion was best demonstrated by the amazing speed with which the original product was put back on the market. There were less than 90 days between Coke's announcement of the replacement of Coke and the return of the original product to the marketplace.

Why was this introduction such a failure? How could the analysis of senior management be so wrong? What did the company overlook? The simple answer to these questions is that the leadership of Coca-Cola, at the time, did not understand the incredible power of influence. They had an influence "tiger by the tail" and did not know what to do with it.

Intelligent Influence Framework

Under Robert Woodruff's leadership, Coca-Cola had done much more than sell a profitable soft drink product. They had developed a corporate and product brand that was so influential it became part of American culture. Consumers grew up with the product and the company's memorable advertisements. They had developed a deep physical, intellectual, and emotional connection to the Coca-Cola product, name, and brand. Instead of a "cult of personality," the company had developed a "cult of product" that influenced the way that people viewed soft drinks, their country, and even themselves.

The introduction of New Coke was, in essence, telling consumers that their lifetime faith in Coke and the Coca-Cola Company was misplaced. An important trust between the company and consumers was broken. For many fans of the product, it was as if the company was telling them to find another religion. As a result, regardless of how the new product tasted, millions of people revolted against this change. The company was forced to do an embarrassing about-face and reintroduce their original product. Much has been written about the failed introduction of New Coke. However, surprisingly, the incredible way in which this incident demonstrated the power of influence has gone unnoticed by most business experts. In the next few pages, I will use Coca-Cola's failed introduction of New Coke to describe each of the components of the *Intelligent Influence Framework*.

Internal Influence at Coke

The passing of Robert Woodruff transformed the *Internal Influence* of Coca-Cola in a way that allowed the leadership, at the time, to change Coke's formula with relatively little internal resistance. While he was alive, Woodruff's incredible influence, even though he was a retired CEO, prevented senior executives from tampering with the company's secret formula.

The executives who decided to introduce the New Coke assumed that old-timers, like Woodruff, did not want any product changes because they were simply living in the past and did not understand the new dynamics of a global technology-driven modern business world. The new leadership ignored the long-term influence-driven culture of the organization and took a chance that their new approach was best for the organization in the long run. Tragically, they did not take the time to learn that the company's corporate culture was the foundation of its long-term success.

External Influence at Coke

Coke's senior leadership did not comprehend the extent of the company's *External Influence*. They did not fully understand the depth with which the company had penetrated the marketplace. They assumed that the demand for Coke was, in economic terms, "elastic" (that consumer demand for the product was very sensitive to the price or taste of the product). These seasoned executives were not aware that they had a *cult of product* that dictated the long-term demand for a product was "inelastic" (that consumer demand was not sensitive to price or taste).

Millions of consumers of Coke and fans of the Coca-Cola Company considered the product and company to be family heirlooms. The homes of many of these fans were decorated with Coca-Cola paraphernalia. Some of these zealots were so connected with the brand they wanted to spend eternity with the product by having their ashes buried in a Coca-Cola can. This gross miscalculation of the company's *External Influence* by senior leadership led to the failed introduction of a product based on its taste and not its influence.

Influence Understanding at Coke

The leadership of Coca-Cola did not take the time to understand either the history of the company or the impact that it had on consumers and culture. If the leadership of the company had effectively analyzed the historical influences of the company (as demonstrated by the corporate culture) and the rationale behind those influences, they would have understood the reasons behind Woodruff's insistence on keeping the same formula for Coke.

If they had done a full assessment of the influence of the company on both consumers and culture, they would have approached the introduction of a new product very differently. Most companies ignore the need for *Influence Understanding* and fail to assess the role of influence in their culture and branding. They, therefore, make the same mistakes that Coke made (albeit without the worldwide attention). It is important to note that this serious mistake can potentially transform profits into significant losses.

Influence Actions at Coke

Clearly, Coca-Cola did not do a good job of assessing their culture and branding. As a result, their actions related to the introduction of the New Coke were a disaster and threatened their position as the #1 company in their industry. The effective use of the *Influence Actions* competencies increases the probability of success of an organization. The ineffective use of these competencies, as in the introduction of the New Coke, guarantees failure.

Influence Awareness at Coke

The Coca-Cola Company decided to introduce the New Coke because they were losing what they considered to be significant market share to Pepsi-Cola and other competitors. The company's market share fell from 24.3% in 1980 to 21.8% in 1984. Each percentage point loss meant a reduction in revenue of approximately $200 million; therefore, this change in market share represented a loss of $500 million to the company. The leadership of the company mistakenly analyzed this loss using purely financial and marketing logic, and determined that it was the taste of the product that was the sole cause of the market share decline. They did not understand the importance of *Influence Awareness* and overlooked the influence of the company's history and the intensified marketing efforts of competitors.

Influence Awareness calls for a thorough examination of the long- and short-term influences that have made a company what it is today. Had Coca Cola's leadership paid attention to the historical reasons for the company's success, they would have understood that the marketplace influence, nurtured by the intensive comprehensive marketing of the company for almost 100 years, was the key to their incredible success. Therefore, changing the formula of the flagship product was not the solution to the company's marketplace challenges.

Since its founding, the Coca-Cola Company has had a unique corporate culture. Coca-Cola was originally developed by John Pemberton in a pharmacy in Columbus, Georgia, in 1886, as a medicine designed to cure disease, eliminate headaches, and even prevent impotence. After a complex series of transactions, Asa Griggs Chandler became the owner of the Coca-Cola Company and formula. He instinctively knew that the company's income was directly related to the amount of advertising the company did.

Chandler, therefore, aggressively advertised the company on billboards and in newspapers (where he gave away coupons for a free Coke at any local fountain). This strategy endeared the company to employees, consumers, and even distributors (community restaurants) because these advertisements generated significant foot traffic for them. This focus on branding had a direct influence on the corporate culture of the organization. Coca-Cola became one of the most productive companies in the country because of the very positive feelings that the advertising generated with employees.

The company's successful marketing efforts influenced both consumers of the product and the general public (especially in the United States) to believe that Coke was much more than a refreshing drink. The company and the product were symbolic of American business, political and military dominance. The successful marketing campaign (using the company's bright red colors, attractive models in advertisements, Santa Claus, and catchy jingles) had influenced much of the world to think that Coke and America were, in many ways, one in the same.

The seemingly sudden change in the formula for Coke was an indication to many that there was not only a problem with the formula, there was a problem with the "American way of life" as envisioned by millions of people. This led to an unprecedented consumer rebellion the likes of which had not been seen before. If the leaders of the company had demonstrated the *Influence Awareness* competency, they would have understood the historical significance of changing the flagship product in the minds of the employees and consumers.

Clearly, there is a direct correlation between soft drink sales and advertising. Prior to the 1980s, Coca-Cola completely dominated advertising for soft drinks. However, Pepsi and Royal Crown (RC) Cola significantly increased their advertising in this decade, thereby reducing Coke's share of the advertising market and, as a result, their share of the market.

This *Influence Awareness* of the direct connection between Coke's dominance of advertising and their share of the market would have convinced the company's leadership to avoid the over-the-top introduction of a revised version of the most successful soft drink in history in its 99th successful year of existence. Instead, to reverse their decline in market share, Coca-Cola would have introduced a product that complements their flagship product and intensified the advertising campaign for both products to increase their market share. Today, this strategy has worked well for Coke and Diet Coke.

Influence Impact at Coke

The second competency and step in the *Intelligent Influence* process is *Influence Impact* and refers to the conscious effort by individuals or organizations to understand how they influence others (individuals, customers, employees, etc.). Successful individuals and organizations assess, in the context of the six types of *Intelligent Influence*, how they are influencing others. They think deeply about the influence that they currently have on their boss, co-workers, subordinates, customers, etc. Likewise, successful corporations identify how they influence their employees, consumers, stockholders, and their industry.

Since its founding, the Coca Cola Company had done a phenomenal job of gaining *Authority Influence* as the #1 soft drink in the world. Their advertising campaign effectively developed *Belief Influence* by convincing consumers to believe that Coca-Cola was as much a lifestyle as it was a beverage. These campaigns also provided the *Inspiration Influence* that motivated consumers to buy the product because of their positive feelings about the brand. They were also swayed by *Reputation Influence* because the company and the product had the most respected brand in their industry. The major investment the company made in a massive marketing campaign demonstrated *Resource Influence*, and the secret formula for Coke demonstrated *Thought Influence*.

At the time of the introduction of the New Coke, the company and product had incredible influence in each of the six types of *Intelligent Influence*. If the leadership of the company examined the organization's *Influence Impact*, they would have understood the extent of their influence and avoided the change to the flagship product which eroded each of these types of influence. Let's examine how the introduction of the New Coke impacted the company's influence in each of these areas:

- *Authority Influence* – The company lost some of its *authority*-related influence because the change to their best-selling product led many to believe that Pepsi had become the #1 selling soda on the market, and Coke was forced to make a change to reclaim the #1 position.

- *Belief Influence* – The product-change led the general public to question their *belief* in the quality of the company and product.

- *Inspiration Influence* – Instead of being *inspired* to purchase Coke, the change *inspired* fans of the company and product to intensely protest the product-change.

- *Reputation Influence* – The *reputation* of the company was damaged because of their ill-advised decision to change their flagship product.

- *Resource Influence* – People questioned whether the company knew how to effectively utilize the *resources* that it had.

- *Thought Influence* – The change to the formula, combined with the fact that they had only developed two products in 99 years, called into question the quality of the company's *thought* leadership.

Amazingly, in the course of one press conference, the company squandered some of the influence they had in each of the six distinct types of influence. When developing corporate strategy, it is essential for a corporation to examine the influence it currently has in each of these six types of *Intelligent Influence* before it develops a strategy for growth. To be successful, corporate strategic planning efforts must be built around these six types of *Intelligent Influence*.

Influence Management at Coke

The third competency and step in the *Intelligent Influence* process is *Influence Management* which refers to an individual's or organization's efforts to control how they are being influenced. The leadership of Coca Cola was facing a major problem. They were losing market share to competitors and wanted to stop the bleeding. If they had taken time to understand the ways in which the company had been influenced historically and the influence of the company in each of the six types of *Intelligent Influence* at the time of the new-product introduction, they would have understood that the problem was not the product—but the marketplace.

In many ways, Coca Cola was hurt by their own success. They had been so dominant for so long that many competitors increased their advertising budgets in an effort to erode Coke's market share. The best-known competitors to Coca-Cola were Pepsi-Cola and RC Cola. However, there were many less-known competitors in the marketplace. The aggressive marketing campaigns of the cola companies were so vicious and aggressive it was called the "Cola Wars."

If Coke had undertaken intensive *Influence Awareness* and *Influence Impact* analysis, they would have understood that the taste of Coke was not the reason for the reduction in market share. Coke's advertising campaigns were so dominant for so long (with little significant competition) that the increasing investment in advertising of Pepsi and Dr. Pepper would naturally erode some of Coke's share of the market. The loss in market share, as a result of these "wars," was inevitable and predictable.

Instead, the problem was the lack of *Thought Influence*. The company had one product for 96 years. They introduced Diet Coke in 1982 as their second product. Frankly, it is amazing that they were so successful for so long with just one product. If leadership had utilized *Influence Management* and invested in marketing Diet Coke and developing a series of new products instead of New Coke, they would have avoided the embarrassing and costly flagship product redesign.

Fortunately, the company learned their lesson and recovered from the failed introduction of the New Coke by focusing on developing and marketing new cola products. Today, because of their strategic *Influence*

Management and *Influence Maximization* efforts, Coke is the #1 cola and Diet Coke is the #2 cola, ahead of Pepsi's flagship product.

Influence Maximization at Coke

The introduction of New Coke limited the company's ability to move toward *Influence Maximization*. As described earlier, the sphere of influence called *Behavioral Influence* is comprised of *Authority Influence* and *Resource Influence*. Coca-Cola lost *Behavioral Influence* because the introduction of New Coke influenced millions of consumers to think that Coca-Cola was no longer the *authority* in the beverage industry and did not have the *resources* of Pepsi.

The sphere of influence called *Rational Influence* is comprised of *Reputation Influence* and *Thought Influence*. Coca-Cola lost *Rational Influence* because the introduction of New Coke hurt Coke's *reputation* with loyal consumers and called into question the *thought* that went into the ill-fated decision to change the leading product in the industry.

Finally, the sphere of influence called *Emotional Influence* is comprised of *Belief Influence* and *Inspiration Influence*. Coca-Cola lost *Emotional Influence* because the introduction of New Coke forced loyal customers to question their *belief* in the product. It also *inspired* its most passionate followers to aggressively fight to ensure that the new product failed. The initial impact on the company's *Caldwell Spheres of Influence*, resulting from the introduction of New Coke, is depicted in the diagram that follows on the next page:

Influence Maximization after the Introduction of New Coke

Behavioral Influence
Coke's "Credibility" as the leading brand in the market was called into question.

Rational Influence
Consumers questioned the "Creativity" of a leadership team that would change the most successful product in the industry

Emotional Influence
Coke lost its "Connection" with a very passionate and loyal customer base.

As the diagram indicates, there is no overlap between the spheres of influence because the introduction of New Coke prevented the company from moving toward a state of *Influence Maximization*. Coca-Cola lost *credibility* with consumers because they questioned the company's status as the industry leader. Loyal customers also questioned the *creativity* of the senior executives who made the decision to alter an iconic product. Finally, Coca-Cola lost the *connection* that it had with its most passionate customers. They felt betrayed because their favorite company turned its back on them by altering their beverage of choice. Fortunately, Coca-Cola brilliantly recovered from the New Coke fiasco by rebranding the original Coca-Cola under the new name "Coca-Cola Classic." This drink was introduced in July of 1985 and, by the end of the year, was outselling Pepsi. In the fall of 1985, Coca-Cola's beverage sales had increased at almost twice the rate of Pepsi's beverage sales.

The leadership of the company not only "dodged a bullet," they were able to transform soda syrup into gold. In reality, the introduction of New Coke helped the company in the long run by revitalizing the brand and publicizing the important place that Coca-Cola held in American life.

Coca-Cola's amazing *Caldwell Spheres of Influence*, after the original Coke was reintroduced, is depicted in the diagram below:

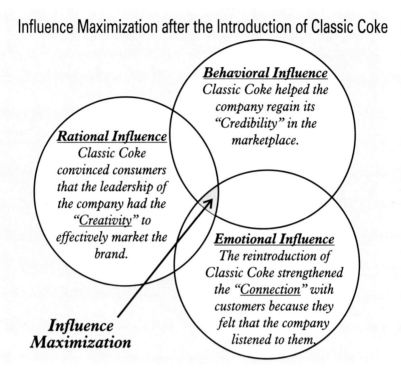

Influence Maximization after the Introduction of Classic Coke

Behavioral Influence
Classic Coke helped the company regain its "Credibility" in the marketplace.

Rational Influence
Classic Coke convinced consumers that the leadership of the company had the "Creativity" to effectively market the brand.

Emotional Influence
The reintroduction of Classic Coke strengthened the "Connection" with customers because they felt that the company listened to them.

Influence Maximization

As the diagram indicates, the space where the three circle overlap is the point of *Influence Maximization*. This is the rare point where a company has achieved extraordinary *Behavioral Influence, Rational Influence,* and *Emotional Influence* in the marketplace. Few companies are able to reach this point. However, the most successful companies are continually striving to achieve this optimal point of influence. Success in business comes from an intense focus on attaining this ultimate (but temporary) state of influence. Many believe that the exact moment when Coke reintroduced Coca-Cola Classic the company had achieved this rare state of *Influence Maximization*.

Coke's brilliant reintroduction of the original Coke was a major success. This strategic move succeeded for three primary reasons. First, it gave the company the *credibility* as the leading brand in the industry once again. Second, the leadership of the company regained its position as one of the most *creative* executive teams in the world. Finally and (in many ways) most importantly, the failed introduction of New Coke strengthened the bond between the company and consumers. The publicity surrounding the change to the formula made it clear to the world that the company had the kind of deep *connection* to consumers that other companies could only dream about. The reintroduction of Classic Coke inspired the most passionate customers to love the company even more because they felt that the leadership heard their complaints and responded to their demands.

Corporate Influence Maximization

Coca-Cola is obviously a very unique company. However, the steps required for a company or individual to increase influence are not unique. Every company that hopes to significantly increase its influence must complete the fourth and final step of the *Intelligent Influence* process which is called *Influence Maximization*. This important step in the strategic use of influence is defined as *"the process of attempting to maximize influence with a targeted group of people."* I recommend that leaders of corporations develop a plan to achieve *Influence Maximization* in their organization by asking the following three key questions:

1) Does the company have the Behavioral Influence or "credibility" necessary to begin the process of maximizing influence?

This question forces corporate leaders to assess whether the company's industry position provides it with the *authority* and access to *resources* necessary to achieve the *credibility* in the marketplace required to achieve its strategic goals. If the company lacks the *Authority Influence* and *Resource Influence* it needs to succeed, it must make the *Internal Influence* investments necessary to increase these two types of influence so that it has the marketplace *credibility* it needs to be competitive.

2) Does the company have the Rational Influence or "creativity" to begin the process of maximizing influence?

Leaders must determine whether or not the company has the *Reputation Influence* or *Thought Influence* necessary to be considered an innovator in their industry. In today's technology-driven global marketplace where change is the only constant, a company's *creativity* is often the difference between success and failure. Companies that do not have a *reputation* as *thought*-leaders are in danger of falling behind their competitors. If the company lacks the *Reputation Influence* and *Thought Influence* it needs to succeed, it must make the *Internal Influence* investments necessary to increase these two types of influence so that it has the marketplace *creativity* it needs to be competitive.

3) Does the company have the Emotional Influence or "connection" necessary to begin to maximize influence?

A company's revenue is driven by the extent to which it *connects* with the people to whom it is selling in its chosen industry. It is, therefore, essential for companies to convince their target markets to *believe* in the company's mission. In addition, companies must focus on *inspiring* their customers to buy from them, instead of their competitors. Corporations that develop *Belief Influence* and *Inspiration Influence* will be in a better position to significantly grow sales because of the strong *connection* that they are able to develop with their customers. If the company lacks the *Belief Influence* and *Inspiration Influence* it needs to succeed, it must make the *Internal Influence* investments necessary to increase these two types of influence so that it has the *connection* with customers that it needs to be competitive.

Individual Influence Maximization

Successful executives intuitively understand how to strategically manage their influence in an organization. However, extraordinary leaders understand that by striving to achieve *Influence Maximization*, they will be significantly more successful than their peers. Their secret of success is based on the answers that they develop to the following three key questions:

1) Do I have the Behavioral Influence or "credibility" necessary to begin the process of maximizing influence in my current position?

A leader must be *credible* in the eyes of the people he or she is attempting to influence. It is essential to be viewed as someone who is qualified, competent, confident, and capable of doing whatever is needed. The leader must be viewed as someone who has either the *authority* and/or the *resources* needed to make the things that are important to the people being influenced happen. If a person lacks the *Authority Influence* and/or *Resource Influence* needed to succeed, he or she must make the *Internal Influence* investments necessary to increase these two types of influence. This is the only way that this particular person will be able to develop *Behavioral Influence* and acquire the *credibility* necessary to begin the process of *Influence Maximization*.

2) Do I have the Rational Influence or "creativity" required to begin the process of maximizing influence in my current position?

Once a leader is seen as being *credible* by the people he or she is attempting to influence, the leader must ensure that these same people consider him or her to be *creative*. It is essential to be viewed as someone who has a solid *reputation* as a respected innovator in his or her area of expertise. The leader must be thought as someone who has either the *reputation* and/or the *brilliance* needed to make the people, being influenced, think about things in new ways. If a person lacks the *Reputation Influence* and/ or *Thought Influence* needed to succeed, he or she must make the *Internal Influence* investments necessary to increase these two types of influence. This is the only way that leaders will be able to develop *Rational Influence* and be viewed as *creative* leaders. This process of developing *Rational Influence* builds on the previous process of developing *Behavioral Influence* and moves further down the path towards *Influence Maximization*.

3) Do I have the Emotional Influence or the "connections" necessary to begin to maximize influence on those people who are important to my professional success?

Once a leader is seen as being *credible* and *creative* by the people he or she is attempting to influence, the leader must make every effort to *connect* with each member of this group. This is extremely difficult because each person likely has very different "hot buttons." Extraordinary leaders have developed the ability to empathize with the individuals they are attempting to influence. They have mastered the first step in the *Intelligent Influence* process, known as *Influence Awareness*, and can quickly develop insight into the ways in which each person they interact with has been influenced. This insight enables them to *connect* with the people they are trying to influence in very deep and powerful ways. This approach enables the leader to get people to *believe* in a project and/or *inspire* them to go above and beyond "the call of duty" because of their strong bond with the leader. However, if the leader lacks the *Belief Influence* and *Inspiration Influence* he or she needs to succeed, the leader must make the *Internal Influence* investments necessary to increase these two types of influence. This is the only way of being able to develop *Emotional Influence* and *connect* with the people the leader is attempting to influence. This process of developing *Emotional Influence* builds on the previous process of developing *Behavioral Influence* and *Rational Influence* and is the final step in moving further down the path towards *Influence Maximization*.

SECTION II

Corporate Influence

CHAPTER 5

Strategic Planning:
The Walt Disney Company

Overview of Section II

In Section I, we examined each of the four steps of the *Intelligent Influence* process. In this section of the book, we will explore ways in which this process has been used by companies to achieve sustainable profitability. We will examine the relationship between three major business disciplines (Strategic Planning, Advertising, and Public Relations), *Intelligent Influence*, and extraordinary organizational success.

As described in the Introduction, Merriam-Webster's Dictionary defines the word *influence* as "*the act or power of producing an effect without apparent exertion of force or direct exercise of command.*" *Influence* has *produced* virtually every important *effect* in the business world. Companies operate the way they operate because of the influence of executives, employees, customers; and the global, economic, and political climate. The exceptional businesses understand that strategically utilizing *Intelligent Influence* is the only way to become an industry leader.

Walt Disney's Early Years

Merriam-Webster's Dictionary defines the word *strategy* as *"a careful plan or method"* and the word *plan* as a *"detailed formulation of a program."* *Influence-Driven Strategic Planning* can, therefore, be defined as *"the effective use of Intelligent Influence strategies to carefully develop a detailed formulation of action steps that position an organization as an industry leader."*

The secret of strategic planning success is the adherence by the leaders of an organization to a core business mission based on the *Intelligent Influence Framework* in the recurring diagram:

Intelligent Influence Framework™

	Internal Influence	*External Influence*
Influence Understanding	*Step 1* **Influence Awareness**	*Step 2* **Influence Impact**
Influence Actions	*Step 3* **Influence Management**	*Step 4* **Influence Maximization**

One of my favorite examples of the importance of staying true to a business mission comes from the story of Walt Disney. This legendary entrepreneur and entertainer was born in 1901 in Chicago and moved to Missouri when he was four years old. Early in his life, Disney was influenced by his relatives, friends, and Midwestern culture to appreciate the importance of having a close family, good friends, and a loving home. In his teenage years, he developed an interest in drawing, entertaining people, and movies. These early interests influenced him to develop an intense fascination with the process of making people happy.

Disney made doing fun things as much a priority in his life as he could and developed a life-long passion for doing entertaining activities (like attending the Electric Park amusement park near his home). He was a child who smiled a lot and derived tremendous enjoyment from making other people smile as well. He came from a family with uncompromising values that went out of its way to help each other. Disney's father farmed with his parents for many years and his uncles Robert and Roy helped his dad financially when he needed help. The Disney clan valued family, friendship, fun, and hard work. This clearly influenced Disney to be a very people-centered, trusting person who, in many ways, was a Pollyanna. His very optimistic view of people and the world led to many failures early in his life. However, it was ultimately the primary reason that he became one of the most successful entrepreneurs in history.

When Walt Disney was in his twenties, his goal in life was to build a company whose mission was to create an art business focused on making people happy. It is often assumed that Walt Disney's path to business success was as magical as his theme parks. However, Disney faced more setbacks than most business people. In spite of facing some tremendous personal and business challenges that would make the average person very bitter and angry, he remained committed to his mission of creating a business that made people happy. He dropped out of high school at a young age and attempted to join the army. However, he was rejected from the army because he was too young. Disney then joined the Red Cross and was sent to France from 1917 to 1918. After returning to Kansas City, he had difficulty finding a job. Fortunately, with the help of his brother, he got a job at the Pesman-Rubin Art Studio where (on a temporary basis) he used his skills as an artist to create advertisements for newspapers, magazines, and movie theatres.

At Pesman-Rubin, he met the talented artist Ubbe Iwerks. They hit it off and decided to form a company called Iwerks-Disney Commercial Artists. Unfortunately, the business failed; and Iwerks and Disney both joined the Kansas City Film Ad Company. Disney decided to open an animation business called Laugh-O-Grams in 1922 with Iwerks and other co-workers at the Kansas City Film Ad Company. In spite of some success in creating popular animated cartoons in and around Kansas City, the business went bankrupt in 1923. Instead of giving up, he developed a new plan for business success.

It is important to note that, for new small businesses, this informal retooling of a business plan can be as effective as the formal strategic planning process used by large businesses today. When you have a visionary entrepreneur, like Walt Disney, this planning can be done on the back of a napkin instead of in an expensive boardroom.

___

Mickey Mouse as a Strategic Plan

The most successful entrepreneurs of all time, like Walt Disney, intuitively recognize that they have to go through a four-step process to reach higher and higher levels of success with innovative new ways. The many business obstacles that Disney faced were, in many ways, "a blessing in disguise." These challenges helped him refine his personal and business mission. He discovered over time that nothing in the world was more important to him than establishing a business that created an entertaining world of animation that made people happy.

With this goal in mind, he moved to Hollywood, California, and in 1923 started a business called the Disney Brothers' Cartoon Studio with his brother Roy. This company was able to generate much needed revenue quickly by selling a series of live-action movies that were combined with animated cartoons created by Disney in the 1920s. This production, called the *Alice Comedies*, was based loosely on the children's book *Alice in Wonderland* and featured a live-action girl with an animated cat named Julius in an animated landscape.

Their second major project was developing an animated series called *Oswald the Lucky Rabbit* that the Disney Brothers created for Winkler Pictures. Unfortunately, Disney was too trusting of his relationship with the company and even his own employees. As a result, in 1928, the CEO of Winkler Pictures hired all of Disney's animators (except Iwerks who would not leave his friend Disney) out from under him, instead of renewing the contract with Disney.

After this deceitful act, the Disney brothers and Iwerks did not panic and give up. They obviously had not heard of the *Intelligent Influence Framework*; however, it is clear that they intuitively went through the strategic-planning process that mirrored the *Intelligent Influence*

Framework. This helped them accurately determine what they needed to do to grow their business. They effectively implemented the following four steps of the process:

Step 1 - Influence Awareness: The Disney brothers and Iwerks reflected consciously (or subconsciously) on their past successes and failures to determine what they needed to do to build a successful business. It was clear that they had a talent and passion for entertaining audiences through stories about animated characters.

Step 2 - Influence Impact: The Disney brothers and Iwerks determined that they had an expertise in developing animated characters that would influence audiences to smile, laugh, and cry. However, they intuitively knew that they did not have the *Authority Influence* and *Resource Influence* required to generate the *Behavioral Influence* (or *credibility*) necessary to position the company as an animation leader in Hollywood. They did not have the *Reputation Influence* and *Thought Influence* required to gain the *Rational Influence* (or *creativity*) essential to establish themselves as industry innovators. Finally, they did not have the *Belief Influence* and *Inspiration Influence* from an entertaining animated character required to generate the *Emotional Influence* (or *connection* with audiences) necessary to generate the revenue needed for the company to survive.

Step 3 - Influence Management: The Disney brothers and Iwerks intuitively knew that the only way that they could get the *credibility*, *creativity*, and *connection* necessary to succeed in the entertainment business was to develop their own animated character. They recognized that there were a number of popular animated cats on the market. They, therefore, decided to make a strategic business decision to build the company around a likable mouse character that they called "Mickey Mouse." The three of them were convinced that this character, if successful, would provide the *Internal Influence* the business needed to generate the *External Influence* (or income) it needed to grow. They bet everything on the hope that Mickey Mouse would enhance the reputation of the business in a way that would lead to significantly greater influence and ultimately revenue for the company.

Step 4 - Influence Maximization: This entertaining mouse did not catch on until the first Mickey Mouse cartoon with sound was produced in

1928 called *Steamboat Willie*. Iwerks drew the mouse, Walt Disney was Mickey's voice, and Roy Disney produced the animated short film. This film was an instant success. Mickey Mouse helped to enable the company to develop the *credibility* they needed to be regarded as one of the leading entertainment companies in Hollywood. This film helped the Disney Company gain a reputation as one of the most *creative* and innovative animation studios in the world. Finally, Mickey Mouse *connected* with audiences in a way that few characters had up to that point in history. By 1930, Mickey Mouse was the most popular cartoon character in the world. Walt Disney, after failing miserably early in his career, had finally created a company that was financially successful. He had the influence in the entertainment world that he had always wanted and was making a lot of people very happy.

Snow White as a Strategic Plan

One of the other characteristics of extraordinarily successful entrepreneurs is that they are never satisfied and are perpetually using a process that follows the *Intelligent Influence Framework* in developing their strategic plans. Walt Disney assumed the role of CEO for the company and made many of the decisions relating to the strategic direction of the company. The success of Mickey Mouse was not enough for Walt Disney. He felt that he was in a great position to influence a wider audience. He, therefore, once again intuitively followed the four-step *Intelligent Influence* process in developing a new business strategy.

Step 1 - Influence Awareness: Disney recognized that the success of Mickey Mouse played an important role in influencing audiences to develop a willingness to see a feature-length animated movie.

Step 2 - Influence Impact: Disney understood that the Mickey Mouse-driven influence of Disney Studios in the early 1930s put the company in a great position to take a chance on producing a feature-length animated film.

Step 3 - Influence Management: Based on his *Influence Awareness* and *Influence Impact* analysis, Disney was convinced that investing in a major feature-length animated movie was worth risking the financial viability of his entire company. However, the so-called experts in the entertainment industry thought that he was foolish to consider risking his entire business on something that had never been done before. Nevertheless, Disney made the investment in a cel- animated feature-length film.

Step 4 - Influence Maximization: The Disney legend grew with the success of his investment in this film. The Disney team created the first major feature-length animated film *Snow White and the Seven Dwarfs* which premiered in 1937. Leaders of the film industry thought that the film would fail miserably and destroy the company. However, Disney stayed true to his strategic mission of creating an animated film that made people happy. This legendary film, which was released to the general public in 1938, maximized its influence on the general public. It grossed an amazing $8 million and became one of the highest-grossing films ever. *Snow White and the Seven Dwarfs* was wildly popular with the public because it had *credibility* garnered from the fact that it was based on a story that everyone knew. It had *creativity* because it was the first cel-animated feature in motion picture history. It *connected* with the audiences because it stimulated their emotions in an entertaining and powerful way.

Disneyland as a Strategic Plan

The profits from this film were used to build the Walt Disney Studios in Burbank, California, in 1939 and was the driving force behind its public offering in 1940. The company built on its success in animation by creating a series of classic films including *Pinocchio, Fantasia, Bambi,* and *Cinderella.* However, the growing competition in the animation industry limited Disney's influence. He, therefore, longed for something new that would enable the company to have even greater influence. Consequently, in the late 1940s, once again, Disney went through the four-step *Intelligent Influence* process in developing yet another strategic plan.

Step 1 - Influence Awareness: The popularity of competing animated characters, like Warner Brothers' Bugs Bunny, combined with the dwindling success of the company's animated films, convinced Walt Disney that he had to enter new markets to regain the global influence that he once had. He could no longer rely on animated films, or the appeal of Mickey Mouse and friends, to fuel Disney's growth. Walt Disney spent a great deal of time reflecting on the positive influence on his childhood that amusement parks had. He remembered how much fun he had going to the Electric Park amusement park near his childhood home. This awareness of influences in his early life helped to convince him that to achieve his goal of making people happy he needed to enter the amusement park business.

Step 2 - Influence Impact: Disney understood intuitively that Mickey Mouse, Donald Duck, Snow White, and Walt Disney Studios gave the company sufficient influence (in each of the six areas of influence) to enable the company to take a chance on creating a theme park based on the Disney characters.

Step 3 - Influence Management: Based on his *Influence Awareness* and *Influence Impact* analysis, Disney was convinced that investing in the creation of Disneyland would grow interest in the studio's characters and significantly increase the influence of the Disney brand. He envisioned creating a place where his characters would come alive, and parents and children could have a lot of fun. Walt Disney, therefore, once again put the company at risk by investing in the development of a theme park on what was once a 160-acre orange grove in Anaheim, California. Once again, the so-called experts thought that Disney was foolish to consider risking his entire business on something that had never been done before. Nevertheless, Disney committed the company to creating Disneyland.

Step 4 - Influence Maximization: Disney had great trouble finding the financing he needed for his dream of an amusement park. He, therefore, created the *Walt Disney's Disneyland* television series to influence the general public and potential financiers of the viability of this project. The idea of this series was brilliant because it provided much needed *credibility* for the idea of an amusement park based on the series. The series demonstrated the *creativity* and forward thinking of the Disney Company. It also *connected* with audiences by bringing together parents and children around Disney-produced entertainment. Disney got the financing he needed and, on July 18, 1955, Disneyland opened with great fanfare.

The amusement park exceeded everyone's expectations and, like the "Walt Disney's Disneyland" television series, provided Disney (the man and company) with the *credibility, creativity,* and *connection* he had hoped for. He built on the park's success by expanding into the production of their first daily television show the *Mickey Mouse Club.* In addition, the studio produced live-action movies in the late 1950s and early 1960s. Disney made very popular movies like *20,000 Leagues Under the Sea, Old Yeller, The Shaggy Dog, Pollyanna, Swiss Family Robinson,* and *The Absent-Minded Professor.*

Walt Disney had a vision for expanding his amusement park empire into Orlando, Florida. He developed the plans for Disney World (which today is the most visited entertainment resort in the world). However, he passed away before the Walt Disney World Resort was opened. By the time Walt Disney died at the age of 65 on December 15, 1966, virtually everything he created had significant influence on the entertainment industry. The Walt Disney Company's animation, television shows, movies, and amusement parks have been phenomenally successful for three key reasons. First, they have the *credibility* that comes from the Disney name. Second, they showcase the *creativity* of the Disney Studios. Finally and most importantly, they *connect* with audiences around the world because of their ability to make people very, very happy. If Walt Disney were alive today, he would likely be very surprised by the size and scope of the global entertainment empire that was made from his simple dream of making people happy.

Intelligent Influence Strategic Planning Lessons

Legendary entrepreneurs and extraordinary CEOs understand that the only way that they will achieve ground-breaking corporate success is to take calculated business risks after going through the *Intelligent Influence* strategic-planning process. It is important to note that the scale of a business's success is directly proportional to the influence of the company and the amount of risk that it takes. The companies that take greater risks are often the first to create new industries or develop wildly popular products and services. Their extraordinary success comes from charting new paths that lead to greater influence and profitability. The four strategic-planning steps that every incredibly successful entrepreneur and CEO takes are as follows:

Step 1 - Influence Awareness: In this step, leaders of the company consciously or subconsciously reflect on the past and current influences in their life (and the life of their business) to develop a better sense of the reasons for both past successes and failures.

Step 2 - Influence Impact: In this step, leaders assess how the business is currently influencing others to determine ways in which it can significantly increase the influence it has over its target audiences. Ideally, this influence assessment is based on a detailed analysis of the extent to which an organization has each of the six types of "Intelligent Influence." However, a general assessment of influence can often be enough.

Step 3 - Influence Management: In this step, leaders seek out the staff, alliances, financing, or consultants needed to overcome the aspects of their corporate culture and business capabilities that are preventing their organization from achieving specific business goals.

Step 4 - Influence Maximization: In this step, leaders are able to lead their organization in a way that enables it to strategically influence their target audience through the perceived Behavioral Influence (credibility), Rational Influence (creativity), and Emotional Influence (connection) of the business.

The corporate leaders who follow this four-step planning process and operate their company according to the resulting plan will be able to achieve the extraordinary success that comes from utilizing the *Intelligent Influence* process in strategic planning. Walt Disney (who failed in business multiple times) successfully followed this approach to strategic-planning success. The good news is that any company of any size should be able to implement this approach as well. The most important ingredient in this process is disciplined visionary CEOs who are willing to surround themselves with senior executives who understand the critical connection between *Intelligent Influence*, strategic planning, and business success.

CHAPTER 6

Advertising: Nike

Reebok's Amazing Growth

For much of the 1980s, Reebok dominated the women's athletic shoe market. Their timing was perfect. They introduced aerobic shoes for women at the very beginning of the aerobic exercise boom. Legend has it that a mistake in the development of the rubber for their shoes enabled them to develop softer more comfortable sneakers. They used this competitive advantage to crush the competition. They dominated the marketplace because their shoes were not only the most fashionable available, they were constructed of soft pliable rubber instead of the rough materials used on their competitor's sneakers.

In just two years, Reebok's 1983 gross sales (driven by this popular line of aerobic shoes originally introduced in 1981) increased 860%. The leadership of the company understood the consumer demand for their products and made the necessary investments in production and staff to increase sales the next year by 500% and another 450% in 1985. Their aerobic shoes established the women's athletic shoe market which, to this day, has become one of the most important consumer markets in the world.

By the mid-part of the decade, Reebok had a passionate following of trendy young consumers with disposable income. They invested more than $5 million dollars in successful advertising that increased consumer demand for their products and enabled them to secure endorsements from well-known celebrities in the sports and entertainment world.

The peak of their advertising influence came a few months after they went public. One of the most popular television actresses in the world at the time (Cybill Shephard) wore a bright orange pair of their shoes under a formal black gown on the red carpet of the Emmy Awards. This was a visible indication of their influence beyond the world of sports. They used this influence to increase company growth by expanding their line of products beyond sportswear to meet general market consumer demand for shoes and clothing in the mid- to late 1980s. Things had never been better for Reebok.

Nike's Decline

In contrast, because of the shift in consumer interest from jogging to aerobics, Nike was losing significant market share in the important U.S. market in the early 1980s. The company sold 50% of the running shoes in the U.S. and grew rapidly during the jogging craze of the late 1970s and early 1980s. However, the drop in demand for running shoes led to their first-ever quarterly drop in earnings in 1983 and 11.5% drop in the domestic sales of their shoes in 1984. In spite of the strong showing of athletes wearing Nike shoes at the 1984 Los Angeles Olympics, Nike's profits were down almost 30%. This poor performance led to significant staff reductions and leadership restructuring in 1985, 1986, and 1987. Things had never been worse for Nike; however, the fortunes of Reebok and Nike would soon change.

Influence-Driven Advertising and Sales™

Merriam-Webster's Dictionary defines *advertising* as the act of *"making something publicly and generally known"* and *"selling"* as the act of *"giving up (a product or service) to another for something of value."* Influence-Driven Advertising and Sales can, therefore, be defined as *"the effective use of Intelligent Influence strategies to make goods or services publicly known in a manner that maximizes the giving up of products or services at a price that generates significant profits for the provider."*

The amazing turnaround of Nike is a model of how to effectively implement *Influence-Driven Advertising and Sales.* They did not know it at the time; however, one of the most successful advertising campaigns in history grew out of Nike's *Intelligent Influence* approach to increasing product sales. The company's leadership had the insight to intuitively follow the steps outlined by the *Intelligent Influence Framework*:

Intelligent Influence Framework™

	Internal Influence	*External Influence*
Influence Understanding	*Step 1* **Influence Awareness**	*Step 2* **Influence Impact**
Influence Actions	*Step 3* **Influence Management**	*Step 4* **Influence Maximization**

Nike founder Phil Knight intuitively utilized an *Intelligent Influence* strategy to engineer the company turnaround. Instead of panicking because of Nike's rapid loss of market share, he led a team of executives who utilized *Influence Awareness* to honestly assess the ways in which they had been influenced as a company. They examined how the changes in the marketplace influenced the company operationally and culturally, and scrutinized the ways in which the company responded to this influence. This analysis indicated that their corporate culture was not innovative enough. When Nike dominated the running shoe market, they assumed that they would always be market leaders and, in short, they got lazy. They lost the culture of innovation which drove their growth in the late 1970s and early 1980s.

Nike's leadership also analyzed the company's *Influence Impact* to identify how the influence of the company on consumers changed as the demand for running shoes declined. They scrutinized the reasons why they were losing market share to Reebok and discovered that they lost influence on customers because they did not change their product line to meet the changing market demands. This analysis gave the company's executive leadership the *Influence Understanding* that they needed to begin the process of plotting a plan for regaining top market share. They knew that internally they needed to reestablish an innovative corporate culture and externally become a brand that more effectively satisfied consumer demand.

Based on their *Influence Understanding*, the Nike leadership team identified the *Influence Actions* they needed to take to regain their lead in the industry. They initiated the *Influence Management* strategies necessary to engineer the company's turnaround. Phil Knight knew that Nike needed to strategically refocus the *Internal Influences* in the company. In 1985, he assumed the post of President and retained his position as Chairman and Chief Executive Officer. Under his leadership, Nike's executive team determined that the company's administrative costs were far too high, their research and marketing operations needed to be consolidated, there was too much unsold inventory on hand, and there were far too many product offerings.

The company, therefore, utilized an *Influence Management* strategy that led to significant cuts in administrative costs, a consolidation of research and marketing operations, a major reduction in warehouse inventory, and the elimination of more than 30% of Nike's shoe offerings. These significant changes provided the *Internal Influences* necessary to increase the productivity of the organization. However, to significantly increase revenue, the company had to utilize *Influence Maximization* strategies that would enable them to have the *External Influence* necessary to sell more shoes than their competitors.

The *Influence Maximization* strategy that Nike used has become one of the most successful in history because it effectively addressed each of the three spheres of influence depicted in the *Caldwell Spheres of Influence* diagram. Nike's successful use of these spheres of influence enabled them to have the *External Influence* on consumers necessary to become the industry leader.

Caldwell Spheres of Influence

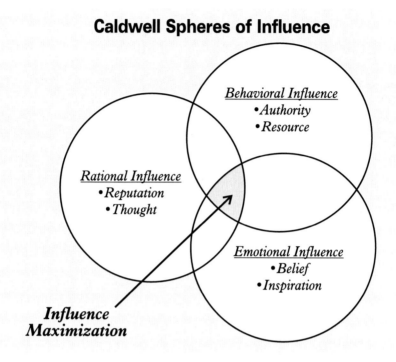

Phil Knight and his leadership team knew instinctively that to regain market dominance they had to have the *Behavioral Influence* necessary to convince large numbers of consumers to make Nike the clear industry leader again. They were focused on influencing customers to purchase Nike products because they were viewed as an extraordinarily powerful company (*Authority Influence*) with the financial resources (*Resource Influence*) to make the highest quality products on the market. They knew that they had to achieve *Rational Influence* by positioning themselves as the most innovative (*Thought Influence*) and admired (*Reputation Influence*) company in the industry.

Nike's leadership understood that they had to gain *Emotional Influence* by developing a consumer-fan base that followed the brand the way fans followed their favorite teams (*Belief Influence*). Finally, they recognized that to dominate the marketplace they had to develop a passionate following of consumers. They did this by convincing potential customers that Nike products were specially designed to help them get the most out of their athletic endeavors. This strategy successfully inspired people to buy Nike shoes (*Inspiration Influence*). This dynamic leadership team intuitively knew that if they strategically utilized their influence to achieve *Behavioral Influence, Rational Influence,* and *Emotional Influence* they would once again dominate the athletic shoe market.

The way that they implemented this *Influence Maximization* strategy has become legendary in the annals of business history. Nike's leadership team conducted extensive research on the consumer marketplace to determine how to influence individuals to buy their products. This analysis indicated that consumers of athletic shoes and sportswear in the late 1980s had an intense inner competitor in them. Whether or not they were great athletes, these consumers all admired those athletes who excelled in their respective sport or career of choice. They each had a deep desire to achieve a little more than they thought they could in both their athletic and personal pursuits. However, most of these athletes and aspiring athletes needed a little push to get the most out of themselves. Nike knew what it had to do to *connect* with these consumers; however, they did not know how to do it.

The answer came in a 1988 meeting with their advertising agency Wieden and Kennedy where it is rumored that Dan Wieden, praising Nike for its unique culture, said, "You Nike guys, you just do it!" It is believed that as soon as those words came out of his mouth, virtually everyone in the room knew that the "Just Do It" slogan was a brilliant catch-phrase for the company. This catch-phrase was perfect for the times because of the appeal that it had to the large numbers of consumers who were intense inwardly focused competitors. These three words, combined with their well-known "swoosh" symbol, provided the framework necessary for the company to have maximum influence in the marketplace.

The leadership of the company recognized that they were well positioned to re-assume market leadership if they executed an influence strategy built around their "Just Do It" slogan. In 1988, they launched a $10 million television campaign around this slogan and increased the budget to more than $40 million in 1989. The phrase "Just Do It" grew to define the *Internal Influence* (culture) of the organization as well as the *External Influence* (branding) of the company. The campaign captured a corporate *belief* in hard work, determination, innovation, and passion that appealed to employees and consumers alike.

The campaign was phenomenally successful from the start and became an advertising legend when they featured sports celebrities like Michael Jordan, Bo Jackson, and John McEnroe. In 1989, Nike led the market with $1.7 billion in sales which grew to an amazing $2 billion in 1990 and $3 billion in 1991. Their focused *Influence-Driven Advertising and Sales* campaign enabled them to once again overtake Reebok as the leading brand in the athletic shoe and apparel market.

The power of effective advertising on *Influence Maximization* was demonstrated by the success of Nike's "Just Do It" campaign and Reebok's failed "Reeboks Lets U.B.U." and "The Physics Behind the Physique" campaigns which never successfully influenced large numbers of consumers behaviorally, rationally, or emotionally. The shift in Reebok's advertising campaigns, combined with the company's loss of market share to Nike, demonstrated a lack of company focus. They seemed to be randomly trying different ads in an effort to find the "Just Do It" branding magic.

Reebok hit bottom when they named a woman's running shoe the "Incubus" and later discovered that in medieval times an Incubus was an evil spirit that was believed to have sex with sleeping women. Fortunately, Reebok, through the development of new shoe technology has continued to grow over the years. However, they have never been able to achieve the branding success of Nike because they have not maximized their *Influence-Driven Advertising and Sales*.

The amazing turnaround of Nike, using *Intelligent Influence* strategies, is just one of many stories of the successful use of *Influence-Driven Advertising and Sales*. To become market leaders, it is essential that companies take the time to assess how they have been influenced (their corporate culture) and how they influence their customers (their corporate branding). This analysis will provide the insight that they need to manage the influences necessary to change corporate culture, increase employee productivity and improve their branding. The intelligent use of influence in this manner is the only effective way to increase product sales. Let's explore the stories behind several other companies that effectively utilized *Influence-Driven Advertising and Sales* to become leaders in their target markets.

A Clear Pattern

Amazingly, every successful advertising and sales campaign in history intuitively utilized an *Influence-Driven Advertising and Sales* strategy built around the *Intelligent Influence Framework*. Every failed campaign did not use this strategy and framework. The stories behind each of these campaigns are unique and interesting. Unfortunately, because of space limitations, all of these stories cannot be presented in this book. However, the important thing about these stories is that they follow the same influence-driven script.

To increase their brand, these extraordinarily successful companies initiate an *Influence Awareness* and *Influence Impact* assessment to get a deeper understanding of their existing corporate culture and brand. This analysis dictates what *Influence Management* they need to implement to develop the corporate culture needed to increase productivity. Finally, the company initiates an *Influence Maximization* strategy built around an advertising and sales campaign that generates the *Behavioral Influence, Rational Influence,* and *Emotional Influence* necessary to develop a brand image that significantly increases sales. This image should be built around the *credibility, creativity,* and *connection* influence strategies discussed in Chapter 4. Companies like Avis, McDonald's, and the Miller Brewing Company have had extremely successful branding campaigns because they followed this unique pattern

Avis, in partnership with the advertising agency Doyle, Dane and Bernbach (DDB), utilized *Intelligent Influence* to develop the "We Try Harder" campaign. This successful campaign influenced consumers to rent from the company in numbers sufficient to turn a $3 million annual loss into a $1 million profit in a year. McDonald's, in partnership with Needham, Harper & Steers (NHS), developed the "You Deserve a Break Today" advertising campaign. This campaign left such an emotional imprint on the minds of consumers that most American adults today think of McDonald's food when they hear the campaign jingle. These two leaders in their respective industries utilized *Intelligent Influence* in their campaign to *connect* with consumers in a way that significantly grew product sales around the world.

The Miller Brewing Company, in partnership with McCann-Erickson Worldwide, utilized *Intelligent Influence* to develop the Miller Lite beer

"Tastes Great, Less Filling" advertising campaign. This campaign utilized sports legends and celebrities that men admired to sell a low-calorie beer to men that previously had no interest in something that was "lite." This campaign increased the sales so significantly that production of Miller beer more than tripled.

Intelligent Influence Advertising and Sales Lessons

Clearly, if Nike, Avis, McDonald's, and the Miller Brewing Company can use an *Intelligent Influence* approach to growing their business, it is highly likely that this approach will help to grow the brand of any business. Obviously, most businesses do not have the resources or brand recognition that most of these companies had before they began the *Influence-Driven Advertising and Sales* process; however, this process can be effective with any organization of any size.

There is a three-stage sales growth pattern that every company goes through. I call this *Sales Influence I*^{TM}, *Sales Influence II*^{TM}, and *Sales Influence III*^{TM}. In the early years of a company's life, it is in the *Sales Influence I* stage where the vast majority of its revenue comes from sales generated by personal relationships. It does not have money to do any formal advertising. It, therefore, influences customers to consider buying its products or services because they like the sales people with whom they interact. At this stage in its life, the company is too new and cash poor to have developed a unique product or corporate-brand identity that will convince potential customers to contact the company without any prior knowledge or contact with sales people.

As the company's sales grow, it is in a position to market its products in a way that enables the use of advertising to develop a product brand. I call this stage *Sales Influence II*. In this stage, companies will start to get customers who buy products simply because they like the product-brand advertising. The company does not have enough money to develop a strong corporate-brand identity. However, it has developed a brand identity for one or more of its products in a specific geographic location that significantly increases sales. The product-brand recognition in its target market is high, even though the company name-recognition is low.

Finally, as they continue to grow, companies enter the *Sales Influence III* stage where they have invested significant money in a corporate branding campaign. These companies have worked with external advisors (management consultants, advertising companies, lawyers, etc.) to develop a unique brand, built on extensive advertising, that enables the company to become a household name in its target market. This branding is designed to significantly increase consumer interest in the company which increases sales of products or services exponentially.

Regardless of the *Sales Influence* stage that a company is in, its leaders will only maximize their revenue through the effective implementation of the *Intelligent Influence Framework*. To increase their sales, all companies must initiate an *Influence Awareness* and *Influence Impact* assessment to get a deeper understanding of their employee productivity and product sales strategy. This analysis dictates what *Influence Management* they need to implement to develop the corporate culture required to increase productivity. Finally, the company initiates an *Influence Maximization* strategy, built around an advertising and sales campaign, that generates the *Behavioral Influence, Rational Influence,* and *Emotional Influence* necessary to develop a brand image that maximizes sales.

There are four fundamental questions that every corporate leader must answer in order to achieve *Influence-Driven Advertising and Sales*. These are the following:

> *1) What have been the major influences in the life of my company, the products we sell, and the people who work for us? (Influence Awareness)*

> *2) How is my company influencing or not influencing potential customers? (Influence Impact)*

> *3) What do I need to do to make my brand significantly more attractive to potential customers? (Influence Management)*

> *4) How do I develop a corporate branding/advertising strategy that will have the "credibility," "creativity," and "connection" necessary to influence people to buy my product or service over those of my competitors? (Influence Maximization)*

The amazing thing about these questions is that they are as applicable to a start-up as they are to a Fortune 500 company. By successfully developing answers to these questions and proactively making the required changes dictated by these answers, companies can significantly enhance their influence in a way that can exponentially increase productivity, sales, and profitability.

CHAPTER 7

Public Relations: Johnson & Johnson

A Tragedy Unfolds

Twelve-year-old Mary Kellerman of Elk Grove Village in Illinois awoke with minor cold symptoms. Later the same day, Adam Janus had minor chest pain while his brother Stanley and sister-in-law Theresa both had headaches. The next day, Mary Reiner, Paula Prince, and Mary McFarland also had minor aches and pains. Amazingly, these apparently common health problems led to one of the most significant corporate public relations crises in history.

Tragically, each of these people died suddenly and mysteriously. At first, the only obvious link between these cases was that all of the individuals were in Illinois at the time of their death. However, within days of the tragedy, it was learned that they each took the same pain relief medicine which contained enough cyanide poisoning to kill a human being instantaneously. The victims, therefore, died very quick deaths.

The Extra-Strength Tylenol that they each ingested for minor aches and pains was manufactured by the Johnson & Johnson Company. For more than a century, this international company, better known as J&J, built a well-deserved reputation as one of the most respected and customer-friendly companies in the world. In 1886, three brothers (James Wood

121

Johnson, Robert Wood Johnson, and Edward Mead Johnson) founded J&J in New Brunswick, New Jersey.

A Legendary History

The company's first claim to fame was publishing the book *Modern Methods of Antiseptic Wound Treatment* in 1888. This publication became one of the premier teaching textbooks for antiseptic surgery and is credited with helping to spread the practice of sterile surgery around the world. In the same year, the company sold the first commercial first aid kits. Their initial target market was railroad workers; however, the kits rapidly became very popular with the general public.

In 1894, J&J successfully entered the childcare market. This was an important year in the company's history because they not only sold popular maternity kits to make childbirth safer for mothers, they also introduced the world famous Johnson's Baby Powder. Over the next two years, they made great strides in improving women's health by developing and marketing the first mass-produced sanitary napkin products for women. In 1898, they introduced the first dental floss to enable average citizens to take better care of their teeth.

Since its founding, J&J demonstrated a strong commitment to philanthropy. They became one of the first national companies to provide major disaster relief support when they provided supplies to Galvaston, Texas, after a devastating hurricane in 1900. The next year, they published the very first *First Aid Manual* which was included in their first aid kits. In 1906, J&J once again demonstrated their commitment to helping others by providing more support than any other company for victims of the 1906 San Francisco earthquake.

James Wood Johnson led the organization from 1910 to 1932 and is credited with building a culture of employee engagement and humanitarian support. In 1920, the Band-Aid® brand adhesives were developed by employee Earle Dickson. These products had the distinction of being the first commercial dressings of small wounds that consumers could apply themselves. Demand for J&J's products grew rapidly around the world. They opened their UK operations in 1924, their Mexico and

South Africa operations in 1930, their Australia operations in 1931, their Argentina and Brazil operations in 1937, their India operations in 1957; and in the 1980s, the company opened important divisions in other parts of the world including Egypt and China.

In 1932, Robert Wood Johnson II became the CEO of J&J and created the global decentralized organization the company operates today. Under his leadership in 1944, the company went public with a listing on the New York Stock Exchange. In 1954, J&J's Baby Shampoo was introduced; and in 1959, the company acquired McNeil Laboratories in the U.S. and Cilag Chemie in Europe. These acquisitions made the company one of the largest pharmaceutical companies in the world. From 1963 to 1973, Philip B. Hoffman served as Chairman and CEO of the company. He handed the company over to James E. Burke who began his tenure as Chairman and CEO in 1976 and served in this role during the Tylenol public relations crisis.

A Major Dilemma

The story of these tragic deaths at the hands of Tylenol spread through media outlets like wild fire. People around the world asked themselves: "How could a well-respected company like J&J, which over the years has saved so many lives, manufacture a product capable of instantly killing people?"

Within days of the deaths, the U.S. Food and Drug Administration (FDA) recommended that consumers avoid Tylenol until the exact cause, scope, and breadth of the danger were determined. The publicity about this crisis put the nation in a state of panic. Hospitals around the country were inundated with calls about Tylenol and potential poisoning. Even though most people avoided Tylenol, no one was completely sure that any over-the-counter products were safe. Consumers felt that if a successful product made by one of the most respected companies in America could contain poison, it is very possible that other well-liked products could pose a serious threat of illness or death.

Tylenol is manufactured by the McNeil Consumer Products division of J&J. As soon as it was determined that Tylenol caused the deaths, this division investigated every aspect of the Tylenol manufacturing process. After painstaking research and analysis over just a few days, J&J and the FDA determined that the quality-control process at McNeil was sufficiently strong to prevent the contamination of the product during the manufacturing process. The research made it clear to both J&J, the FDA, and law enforcement that one or more people purchased the product in several stores in Illinois, laced a few of the individual capsules with cyanide, and returned the product to store shelves.

James Burke was faced with one of the most difficult public relations decisions any CEO has ever had to face. The wrong corporate response could permanently damage the company's reputation. In addition, J&J was seriously at risk of losing its most profitable product. Many marketing experts predicted that the Tylenol brand (which accounted for almost 17% of the company's net income) could never recover from this public relations nightmare. Some of these experts even believed that the J&J brand could never recover.

Influence-Driven Public Relations™

It was clear that J&J was not at fault for these tragedies. Burke, therefore, could have legitimately stated publicly that "J&J is saddened because of the loss of life; however, because we bear no responsibility for these deaths, we will continue to sell Tylenol throughout the world." Instead, he and his leadership team intuitively utilized the *Intelligent Influence* process in developing a strategy for responding to this crisis. Merriam-Webster's Dictionary defines *public relations* as *"the business of inducing the public to have understanding for and goodwill toward a person, firm, or institution." Influence-Driven Public Relations* can, therefore, be defined as *"the effective use of Intelligent Influence strategies to develop public goodwill toward an organization."* J&J's *Influence-Driven Public Relations* response to the crisis followed the *Intelligent Influence Framework* shown in the diagram:

Intelligent Influence Framework™

	Internal Influence	External Influence
Influence Understanding	**Step 1** **Influence Awareness**	**Step 2** **Influence Impact**
Influence Actions	**Step 3** **Influence Management**	**Step 4** **Influence Maximization**

Influence Awareness

When Burke first learned about the crisis, he quickly formed a seven-member leadership strategy team to develop a crisis response strategy. He led the team in an exercise of *Influence Awareness* where they revisited the history of the company and the influences that made J&J successful. The most important of these influences was the company's credo, which was and still is as follows:

Johnson & Johnson Credo

> *We believe our first responsibility is to the doctors, nurses and patients, to mothers and fathers and all others who use our products and services. In meeting their needs everything we do must be of high quality. We must constantly strive to reduce our costs in order to maintain reasonable prices. Customers' orders must be serviced promptly and accurately. Our suppliers and distributors must have an opportunity to make a fair profit.*

We are responsible to our employees, the men and women who work with us throughout the world. Everyone must be considered an individual. We must respect their dignity and recognize their merit. They must have a sense of security in their jobs. Compensation must be fair and adequate, and working conditions clean, orderly and safe. We must be mindful of ways to help our employees fulfill their family responsibilities. Employees must feel free to make suggestions and complaints. There must be equal opportunity for employment, development and advancement for those who qualify. We must provide competent management, and their actions must be just and ethical.

We are responsible to the communities in which we live and work and to the world community as well. We must be good citizens — support good works and charities and bear our fair share of taxes. We must encourage civic improvements and better health and education. We must maintain in good order the property we are privileged to use, protecting the environment and natural resources.

Our final responsibility is to our stockholders. Business must make a sound profit. We must experiment with new ideas. Research must be carried on, innovative programs developed and mistakes paid for. New equipment must be purchased, new facilities provided and new products launched. Reserves must be created to provide for adverse times. When we operate according to these principles the stockholders should realize a fair return.

Even though this credo was crafted by Robert Wood Johnson (the Chairman of J&J from 1932 to 1963) in 1943, it played an important role in influencing how the Burke leadership team responded to the Tylenol crisis. This credo convinced the team that it was essential to stay true to the company's early influences and put customers first.

Influence Impact

The second step that the leadership team took was to examine the *Influence Impact* of the crisis. It was clear that, because of the product tampering, the company lost significant influence in each of the six areas of influence. J&J lost *Authority Influence* because the public no longer considered the company to be the leading authority on health and safety. They no longer had the same level of *Resource Influence* because people questioned the resources of a company that could not prevent the release of deadly products. The company no longer had *Reputation Influence* because they lost their reputation as the company that was most concerned with the well-being of their customers. J&J lost *Thought Influence* because they were no longer thought of as one of the most innovative companies in the world. They lost *Belief Influence* because many customers no longer believed in the J&J brand. Finally, the company lost *Inspiration Influence* because many consumers lost their emotional connection to the brand (having been used by their parents and parent's parents, etc.).

Influence Management

They, therefore, implemented the third step of the process and developed an *Influence Management* plan that would enable the company to regain influence in each of the six areas of influence. Their strategy worked brilliantly. The initial discussion of the leaders was focused on answering two very important questions. The first question was "How do we protect people in this crisis?" The second question was "How do we save Tylenol?"

The very first thing that they did was to tell consumers not to purchase the product until the company could guarantee the complete safety of consumers. In addition, they stopped all advertising and production of the product. No healthcare company of J&J's size had ever told consumers not to purchase a product. Then, in an even more significant move, they ordered a national recall of every capsule on the market. This *Intelligent Influence* approach to the crisis helped to reestablish the influence that J&J lost when the crisis went public. They were able to regain each type of influence in a way that enabled them to achieve *Influence Maximization*.

Influence Maximization

J&J's *Influence Maximization* strategy enabled them to regain both market share and their position as one of the most trusted companies in the world. They effectively utilized the *Caldwell Spheres of Influence* depicted in the diagram below. J&J's public-relations approach was brilliantly designed to maximize their sphere of *Behavioral Influence* by establishing the public *credibility* of the company; *Rational Influence* by demonstrating *creativity* in their approach to addressing the crisis; and *Emotional Influence* by *connecting* with consumers by showing them that the company cared about their well-being.

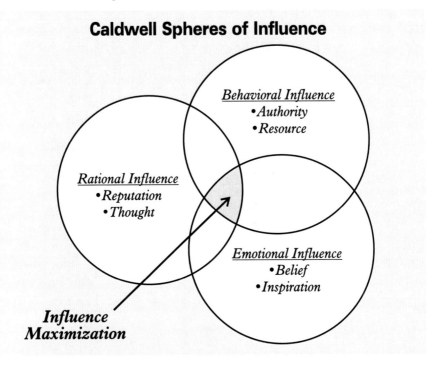

J&J's sphere of *Behavioral Influence* was obtained by re-establishing *Authority Influence* and *Resource Influence*. They regained *Authority Influence* by taking a leadership role in addressing the crisis. They demonstrated *Resource Influence* by showing the general public that they had the financial resources to withstand the millions of dollars of losses they would sustain by recalling their flagship product.

Their sphere of *Rational Influence* grew because of J&J's ability to regain their *Reputation Influence* and *Thought Influence*. They regained *Reputation*

128

Influence by demonstrating that protecting the public was more important than making money. They benefitted from *Thought Influence* because they were the first company of their type to take the bold and creative move of recalling their best-selling product. In addition, they demonstrated their ability to be innovative by quickly developing tamper-proof packaging for their products.

The company's sphere of *Emotional Influence* was expanded because of their ability to demonstrate *Belief Influence* and *Inspiration Influence*. They regained *Belief Influence* because their actions influenced many customers to regain their belief in the J&J brand. Finally, the company's actions led to an increase in *Inspiration Influence* by re-establishing the emotional connection that many customers had to the brand.

One of the challenges of reviewing successful CEO strategies is that the natural tendency of readers is to minimize the significance of a leader's actions in a time of crisis. It is clear, in hindsight, that Burke did the right thing. The faulty assumption is that responding to crises should be much easier for CEOs now that they have the Burke model. Unfortunately, even today, most CEOs ignore the lessons learned from Burke and his leadership team's actions. Amazingly, even the J&J leaders who succeeded Burke failed to follow Burke's successful strategy in managing some of the crises the company has faced recently.

Intelligent Influence Public Relations Lessons

J&J CEO James Burke's success in dealing with one of the most difficult crises facing any CEO, at any time, should serve as a model for other CEOs. There are four fundamental questions that CEOs (regardless of the size of the organization that they lead) must answer in order to achieve *Influence-Driven Public Relations*. These are the following:

1) What influences have led to the financial success and revenue growth in the company to date? (Influence Awareness)

This question helps CEOs and the public relations professionals with which they work begin the process of connecting the history of the company with the public relations issue they are addressing.

2) How is the company currently influencing (positively or negatively) customers? (Influence Impact)

This question enables company leadership (as directed by the CEO) to identify the current influence-related strengths and weaknesses of the company (using the six types of *Intelligent Influence*). The answer to this question helps to explain the reasons why a public relations issue has surfaced in the first place.

3) What is the company doing to have a greater positive influence on customers and the general public? (Influence Management)

This question tells a target audience what the company is doing (or planning to do) about the particular public relations issue.

4) What is the company doing to enable it to be extraordinary and have the Behavioral Influence (credibility), Rational Influence (creativity), and Emotional Influence (connection) that will influence large numbers of people to buy products or services over those of its competitors? (Influence Maximization)

This question is frequently missed by CEOs and the public relations professionals with which they work. The public relations communication must be designed to demonstrate the *credibility* of the company and its CEO. If this credibility is not established, the audience will not listen to the message. The public relations message must be somewhat *creative* to demonstrate that a great deal of thought went into the message. Saying the same old thing, in a new way, will not engage an audience. It is essential that there is something original and thought-provoking in the message. Finally, the message must connect with the target audience so that they have an emotional *connection* with what is being said by the CEO or the public relations executive.

If the CEO and the public relations professionals with which they work can answer each of these four questions in a way that helps them develop a message that appeals to their target audience, they will have attained *Influence-Driven Public Relations*.

SECTION III

Individual Influence

CHAPTER 8

Leadership:
Princeton University

Overview of Section III

In Section I, we examined in detail each of the four steps of the *Intelligent Influence* process. In Section II, we explored the ways in which this process has been used by corporations to achieve success in three of the major corporate business disciplines. In this section of the book, we will examine the relationship between three major people business disciplines (Leadership, Sales, and Diversity), *Intelligent Influence,* and extraordinary individual success.

Influence has *produced* virtually every important *effect* in the success of business executives. Accomplished individuals in business do what they do and think the way they think because of the influence of their supervisors, co-workers, subordinates, customers, family, friends, and society. Whether or not they have heard the term, exceptional executives intuitively understand that strategically utilizing *Intelligent Influence* is the only way to become extraordinarily successful in a business career.

Discovering My Leadership Skills

Over the years, I have studied many stories of executives who strategically used influence to become successful. In this chapter, I have chosen to use the personal story of my leadership experience at Princeton because it follows the same pattern of success used by corporate leaders. My audiences have appreciated this story because it contains the elements common to every story of business leadership success. Most importantly, since I lived this story, I can draw a very direct connection between leadership success and *Intelligent Influence.*

When I was a freshman at Princeton University, the men's tennis team was one of the top ten teams in the United Sates. The coach, David Benjamin (who was one of the best college tennis coaches in the country), did a tremendous job of recruiting top players to come to the program. Our #1 player, Jay Lapidus, was a rival of John McEnroe as a junior and one of the best players in the country. He was so talented that he eventually became a top 50 professional player. Leif Shiras, one of the lower-ranked members of the team when I was a freshman, improved enough after Princeton to be a top 50 professional player and reach the fourth round of Wimbledon. He has since become one of the most respected tennis announcers in the world. The team was so good that all the other starting players on the team were talented enough to play on the professional tennis circuit.

I was a sectionally ranked player in high school who rarely had a chance to take lessons or practice with top players. I had not played any national junior tournaments and was not one of the highest-ranked players in the country, so I was not recruited to play on the Princeton Varsity A team. However, I knew that I had talent because I had briefly attended a camp with some of the best players in the country, run by Harry Hopman (who many consider the best tennis coach in history) and proved that I had the talent to be a top national player with the right coaching.

Even without coaching, I was good enough to play on the Varsity B team which was better than many Varsity A teams in the country. Unfortunately, it was coached by someone who knew very little about competitive tennis and, for some reason, consistently played players that I had beaten in challenge matches ahead of me. I wasn't sure if it was because he did not like the way I hit the ball or because I was the only player of color on the team. Nevertheless, as an insecure urban black kid just out of high school, I did not have the nerve to confront him or complain about the situation. I just decided to quit the team my sophomore year and spend my time elsewhere at Princeton.

As a United States Tennis Association (USTA) board member, I now have a chance to play with some of the best tennis players in history. Knowing what I know now about professional tennis players, it was a tragedy that I did not have a good coach at Princeton. I have learned that had I had the right Varsity B coach at Princeton, there was a good chance that I would have played Varsity A tennis at Princeton. I also might have had a chance to play on the professional tennis circuit. Unfortunately, I now know that the decision to leave the team had more of a detrimental impact on my tennis playing career than I realized at the time.

The point of my college tennis story is that everyone, at one time or another, faces obstacles in life that seem to be unfair. The key is not to let these obstacles influence you in a negative way. Too many people succumb to negative influences and lose confidence in their abilities. Life is filled with both challenges and opportunities. True leaders recognize that when one door of opportunity closes, others open up.

I have had the good fortune of learning over the years that "good things often come from bad circumstances." When I decided to leave the tennis team, I focused on making money (to supplement my financial aid) by working more intensely as a student worker in the Commons Dining Halls. My bad experience on the tennis team turned into a great leadership experience. "Commons," as the dining hall complex was officially known, was the largest eating facility on campus. This massive place had four large dining halls and served over 20,000 meals a week. The unique thing about Commons was that the checking-in, serving, and cleaning up were done entirely by students. There were over 400 students who worked part-time at Commons to pay for college and earn some extra money.

My first job at Commons was mopping the dining hall floors. At the time, I was a shy insecure kid who enjoyed working alone. I really liked this job because I could make good money cleaning the floors by myself several times a week. However, when I learned that I could make more money as a crew captain, I decided to pursue this position (even though

135

I was an introvert who had no experience managing people). I decided to push myself beyond my comfort zone and focus on doing whatever it took to be promoted. My hard work paid off and I was promoted to the position of crew captain. This leadership position required that I manage up to seven student workers during a meal.

To my surprise, I discovered that I had a unique ability to lead people and became one of the most popular crew captains in the dining hall. My success in this role gave me the confidence to apply for a student manager position. Only seven people out of the 400 workers were selected for this prestigious position. These leaders were each assigned one to three full meals a week and were ultimately responsible for every aspect of the meal (except cooking the food). In addition, they were the senior leadership team responsible for managing payroll, scheduling, strategy, and human resources. Best of all, they made considerably more money than any of the crew captains.

My success as a crew captain influenced me to have confidence in my leadership abilities. This newly found belief in myself helped me to earn the coveted promotion to the student manager position. As I think back to this accomplishment, I still do not know how I succeeded in a virtually full-time job at Commons while managing a very demanding Princeton course load (which included taking more courses than most students). I was so successful as Student Manager that I was promoted to the position of Student Coordinator (which was the highest-ranking student job on campus). In this position, I was the Chief Executive Officer (CEO) of the 400-person strong student food service workforce. I, therefore, represented the entire student body when it came to issues of food service, administration, and employment on campus. I even had a chance to represent the student body when Princeton was considering the possibility of changing its structure to a college system similar to the one in place at Harvard and Yale.

My Commons experience played an important role both in my gaining acceptance to the Wharton MBA program and succeeding in business. I will never forget how I was able to turn my devastating experience on the Princeton tennis team into extraordinary leadership success. As I reflect on my first significant leadership experience, I realized that my rise from the position of janitor to CEO at Commons was driven by the subconscious use of the *Intelligent Influence Framework* as depicted below:

Intelligent Influence Framework™

	Internal Influence	External Influence
Influence Understanding	Step 1 **Influence Awareness**	Step 2 **Influence Impact**
Influence Actions	Step 3 **Influence Management**	Step 4 **Influence Maximization**

Influence Awareness

I did not pay much attention to the fact that, as I was climbing the ladder at Commons, I reflected (almost daily) on the many positive and negative influences in my life. As described in Chapter 1, I call this self-reflection *Influence Awareness* and, for individuals, define it as *"the process of understanding the most significant ways in which a person has been influenced in the past and how one is currently being influenced."* My dad is a retired United Methodist minister who, as was the case with Methodist ministers at the time, moved every five or so years. I was born in Boston and lived in the African-American section of the city called Roxbury. My parents did not have a lot of money but they wanted my brother Paul and me to have the best education available, so they struggled to pay for us to attend the prestigious Advent School in the Beacon Hill section of the city. It was in Roxbury and at Advent that I began a challenging dual life where I felt "too white" in Roxbury's black community and "too black" in Advent's white student community.

My dad got a job in New York as the Executive Director of the Ministerial Interfaith Association of Harlem. I therefore attended 2nd through 7th grades living mostly in the African-American section of New York called Harlem and attended the prestigious predominantly white Cathedral School of St. John the Divine near Columbia University. Once again, I never felt comfortable developing very close friends because I felt "too white" in Harlem and "too black" at Cathedral. I was a good basketball player which enabled me to gain the respect of my peers in Harlem and a good tennis player which enabled me to get the respect of my peers at Cathedral. Sports served as the foundation from which I developed the ability to get people of any race or background to like me on a superficial level. However, I had an invisible protective wall and never felt comfortable letting anyone outside of my family get too close to me.

My dad took a position as Senior Pastor at the First United Methodist Church in New Haven, Connecticut, so we moved to New Haven. My parents once again made some amazing financial sacrifices and sent my brother and me to the prestigious Hopkins School where I was one of two black students in my class. However, this time we lived in a predominantly white, middle-class neighborhood. Once again, I developed a lot of good friends. However, I never dated or had anyone that I would consider my best friend because of my insecurities.

As the son of a minister, I was a member of the "first family" of many different churches. My dad served as pastor of eight different churches as I was growing up. More than 90% of the members of four of the churches were white and more than 90% of the members of the other four churches were black. I, therefore, learned how to be a diplomat and represent the family and church well in many very diverse environments. Early on, I developed an ability to quickly find things to talk about that were of interest to anyone at anytime. Most importantly, I developed a fascination in learning about the ways that people were influenced. Over time, I developed the unique ability to see things from the perspectives of very different people. It has now become very clear that this challenging environment helped me develop a heightened sense of empathy.

My childhood and youth forced me to develop the ability to engage anyone in an entertaining conversation without revealing anything about my true feelings. However, unlike many politicians, I had a genuine interest in the background and perspectives of other people. I learned never to assume anything about anyone based on stereotypes because people do what they do because of the influences in their lives (not because of other superficial things like their race or religion). My unusual youth clearly fueled my passion for studying influence 30 years later.

Anyone who has managed a food service operation knows that there is no business that is more chaotic than running a restaurant during a meal. The restaurant business is among the fastest, most intense, and chaotic of any business. Customers (especially busy academically focused students) want to sit down and get their food quickly without any hassles. The food service leaders who are successful are those who can solve problems immediately and get the meal staff to like, respect, trust, and follow them during the chaos of a meal. I realized that the skill of getting very different people to like me quickly (that I learned in my awkward youth) was the key to my success at Commons. I also recognized that as I became successful in one level at Commons, I was influenced to develop the confidence in my leadership skills that I needed to get to the next level in the organization.

Influence Impact

The second step on my ladder to success at Commons was *Influence Impact*. This step, as described in Chapter 2, is defined as *"the process of understanding the most significant ways in which a person currently influences others and the areas of influence where improvement is needed."* I had no idea, at the time, that there were six distinct types of *Intelligent Influence*. However, intuitively, I was able to assess the extent of my influence in each of the following areas:

- *Authority Influence* – The Commons Dining Halls student workforce had a very hierarchical structure. The first level was called "crew worker." The second level was called "crew captain." The third level was called "student manager" and the highest ranking student worker on campus was called "student coordinator." As I worked my way up the ladder from worker to captain to manager to coordinator, I was amazed by the increasing intensity of *Authority Influence* that I had.

The students at Princeton seemed to have great respect for people in authority positions and did an amazing job of following the direction of the people leading their work teams. Over the years, I have learned that virtually everyone, no matter how smart or accomplished, is looking for someone to lead in areas outside of his or her expertise. People naturally get frustrated when someone, who claims to be an expert in an area, does not utilize their *Authority Influence* to make things happen. The students at Commons had great respect for the people who were able to provide clear direction to the work teams. Unfortunately, they had little respect for those who did not know how to use this influence to lead a team.

- *Belief Influence* – As one might imagine, the Princeton students working in the Commons Dining Halls were more focused on their school work than they were on working in the dining hall. To most of them, it was just a job they needed to do to make some extra money. I was, therefore, faced with the difficult task of making them believe that what they were doing was important. I did this by demonstrating a commitment to excellence in my work that became contagious. The competitive nature of Princeton students motivated them to match my commitment to excellence. As a result, the people who worked for me went "above and beyond the call of duty" because they *believed* in doing the best job possible.

- *Inspiration Influence* – One of the most important things that I learned in my youth is that everyone likes to laugh. My experience in supervisory roles at Commons taught me how to strategically use humor to inspire people to want to help me become successful. Through humor and the appearance of not taking myself too seriously, I was able to create project teams that were both fun and productive. The use of *Inspiration Influence*, through humor, helped me become one the most sought after supervisors on campus.

- *Reputation Influence* – My parents influenced me to do a lot of things. However, one of the most valuable things that I learned from my parents was to treat everyone with tremendous respect. This served me well at Commons. I was surprised to learn that most of the students working in the dining hall were selective in demonstrating respect. They were warm and friendly to the people they liked, and cold and distant to others. I made sure that everyone on my team felt the great respect that I had for them. I also went out of my way to let them know that I was grateful for their help and support. This approach to leadership increased my influence by enabling me to develop a reputation among the workers at Commons as a great person and a fantastic boss.

- *Resource Influence* – As a manager and eventually the student coordinator, I had tremendous control over the student workers' schedules. I led the team of student managers who determined each student's schedule, how many hours they worked, and their income. This *Resource Influence* was the primary reason that students treated those of us who were student managers (even though they were their peers as students) as if they were the Board of Directors of a Fortune 500 company.

- *Thought Influence* – I learned early in life that I get bored very, very easily. The only way that I can maintain interest is to think of doing things in a unique and different way. This trait sometimes did not serve me well in school (which often penalized creativity and rewarded memorization). However, this weakness in school has become a strength in business. It has enabled me to come up with many new and creative ideas. I made a special effort to be creative at Commons. I was constantly trying to figure out new and different ways to mop floors, and redesign the process of serving and cleaning up after a meal. When I was the student coordinator, I single-handedly took the very bold step, at the time, of convincing the Princeton University administration to move the vegetarian dining hall so that the configuration of the four dining halls was better for students. I gained a great deal of *Thought Influence* because my new ideas were very well received by both the students and the administration.

Influence Management

I was able to have the *Influence Impact* described above by making a special effort to learn from others how to become a more effective and influential leader at the Commons Dining Halls. I intuitively utilized the process of *Influence Management* which, as described in Chapter 3, is defined as *"the intentional effort by a person to utilize a developmental plan designed to strategically increase one's External Influence."* I subconsciously conducted the analysis depicted in the *Individual Influence Management* box below:

Individual Influence Management

Personality Type (P) + Skills (S) + Internal Influence (I) = External Influence (E)

Where the symbols represent the following:

P = The personality type of an individual.

S = The skills and abilities a person possesses.

I = The developmental influence action (training, coaching, team building, etc.).

E = The ways in which this person influences others as a result of their actions.

When I first started working at Commons, I enjoyed working alone. I actually looked forward to the opportunity to mop the floors of a large dining hall by myself. I was an introvert who lacked self-confidence. However, I had the very valuable skill of an intense work ethic. I was clearly one of the hardest student workers on staff. When I decided that the *External Influence* that I wanted was to influence people to promote me to the position of crew captain, I asked for help and guidance of several mentors who were successful crew captains. I knew that I needed the type of coaching (*Internal Influence*) that would help me overcome my introverted insecure personality and build on my work-ethic skills. Fortunately, these individuals provided the precise *Internal Influence* that I needed to prepare me for the interviews (which consisted of several senior managers observing me managing a crew of students as they either prepared for, served, or cleaned up after a meal).

One of the most important things that I learned at Commons was the difference between a mentor and a sponsor. Mentors are those who can provide valuable career guidance and advice; however, they are not in a position to make the decision as to whether or not you are promoted or receive a raise. Sponsors are those who are in a position to make a decision (or part of the team making the decision) on your career. I was smart enough at this early stage in my career to find senior-manager sponsors who liked me and knew my capabilities (largely because I provided great value over the years to project teams that they managed). I intuitively knew that the best way to get the support of sponsors is to become an invaluable member of a team they lead.

This *Internal Influence* strategy paid off. The advice I received from my mentors and support for my promotion from sponsors enabled me to counter my introverted personality and build on my work ethic and get the promotion to crew captain. I went through an even more intense process a year later as I competed for the position of senior manager. It was clear that my ability to make superficial friends and keep the people on my project team engaged, while exceeding expectations, was a valuable skill at Commons. However, I remained introverted once the work of my project team was done. I did not feel comfortable hanging out with the people I worked with. It was clear that a key skill of good senior managers was that they had to be perceived as being extroverted before, during, and after work.

To prepare for the much more intense senior-manager interviews (which consisted of senior managers watching me run an entire meal), I identified three senior managers to be both mentors and sponsors. These very experienced individuals helped me overcome my personality weaknesses and build on my skills to get the promotion to senior manager. I was selected to be the CEO of the dining hall largely because I was able to get the retiring student coordinator to serve as a mentor and sponsor, and provide the *Internal Influence* that I needed to win a very close competition for this coveted position with one of the other senior managers. As I reflect on the promotions I received at Commons, I intuitively was able to fully utilize the *Individual Influence Management* equation. I was able to find the *Internal Influence (I)* that I needed to help me get the most of my *Personality (P)* and *Skills (S)* to achieve the *External Influence (E)* that I wanted. This process is not an easy one. However, it is the development process that is used intuitively by every successful leader.

Influence Maximization

I have described in detail the process that I went through to get promoted at Commons. However, I have not discussed whether or not I was a success in my role as CEO of the Commons Dining Halls. It is very clear that timing plays an important role in increasing the influence of extraordinary leaders. President Franklin Delano Roosevelt was the only four-term U.S. President because the Great Depression and World War II influenced the country to stay with the same leader for multiple-presidential terms. There are a lot of extraordinary business leaders; however, the best-known business leaders become legends because the companies that they lead make products that transform society: Henry Ford and automobiles; Bill Gates and computer operating systems; John Pierpont Morgan and banking; Steve Jobs and the iPod, iPhone, and iPad. Most successful leaders never become legends; however, the level of their success is driven by the timing of their tenure as leaders.

My experience at Commons obviously does not compare to the extraordinary success of these icons of leadership. However, like them, timing played an important role in determining the extent of my influence. The success of my tenure as the CEO of Commons benefitted from the timing of some of the proposed changes at Princeton University at the time. As the third oldest university in the Ivy League, the leadership at Princeton (founded in 1746) often examined what they considered to be best practices at their older rivals Harvard University (founded in 1636) and Yale University (founded in 1701). Both Harvard and Yale structured student life around a House and Residential College system respectively. This structure forced students to spend the majority of their social time with members of their house or college. The belief was that this system would provide students with a more intimate college experience. However, one of the reasons that I decided to attend Princeton University was the open college system that did not limit student interaction. Instead, students were free to live where they wanted to and interact with a broader group of students. This structure fit my personality (and the early influences in my life) very well. I could get to know a lot of people pretty well, instead of a few people intimately.

When I became CEO of the Commons Dining Halls, Princeton was considering the possibility of making the historic change to a college system like the one in place at Yale. This change would eliminate Commons as a campus-wide dining hall providing 20,000 meals a week. Instead, the university would establish much smaller dining halls connected to the small colleges throughout the campus. As the highest ranking and most influential student worker on campus, I represented the student workers in discussions on establishing a campus-wide college system at Princeton. At the time, Princeton had a very strong Princeton student work force where students made money by meeting the food service and other needs of students on campus.

The proposed college system would severely limit the employment opportunities for students on campus. The smaller college system would eliminate jobs and prevent hundreds of students from earning extra tuition money by working in the dining halls. I made it very clear that students did not want this change and had surprising success making my case to the administration. I knew that I had real influence and that my argument was gaining traction when one of the senior administrators "jokingly" tried to persuade me to change my mind by offering to put a brass plaque, with my name and likeness, in the main Commons dining hall if I supported the implementation of the college system.

It is hard to prove why the change to the college system seemingly took longer than originally planned. I recognized that the university would likely never admit that students delayed their plans. However, I certainly played an important role in influencing the administration's planning of the college system (which interestingly did not take place until after I graduated in 1982). At the time, I did not understand how, as a lowly student, I was able to influence the powerful Princeton University administration until I discovered the amazing power of *Intelligent Influence.*

The secret of my influence was that I was unknowingly able to effectively utilize *Influence Maximization* as depicted in the diagram that follows on the next page:

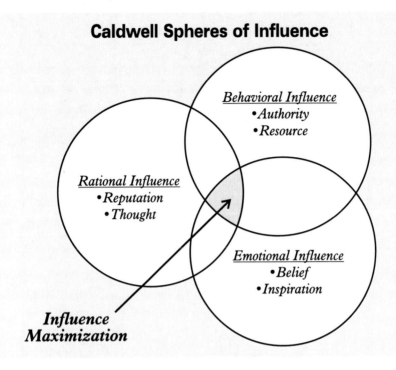

Caldwell Spheres of Influence

Behavioral Influence
- *Authority*
- *Resource*

Rational Influence
- *Reputation*
- *Thought*

Emotional Influence
- *Belief*
- *Inspiration*

Influence Maximization

The university was forced to hear my case because I was able to use each of the three *Caldwell Spheres of Influence*. I utilized the sphere of *Behavioral Influence* by demonstrating both *Authority Influence* and *Resource Influence*. As the leader of the largest student workforce on campus, I had the *Authority Influence* that comes from holding the highest student position on campus. I also had *Resource Influence* because I possessed the power to mobilize 400 students to communicate their displeasure with the plan.

I utilized the sphere of *Rational Influence* by demonstrating both *Reputation Influence* and *Thought Influence*. My *Reputation Influence* emanated from the perception of others that I was honest, an effective leader of Commons, and was able to work very well with university staff. My *Thought Influence* grew largely out of my innovative and successful operational redesign of dining hall operations rooted in the unique changes to the vegetarian dining hall.

I utilized the sphere of *Emotional Influence* by demonstrating *Belief Influence* and *Inspiration Influence*. My *Belief Influence* was based on my argument that students who needed to earn money to pay a significant portion of their tuition would be hurt by the new plan. I was able to get both students and administrators to believe that this was a significant problem with the residential college plan. My *Inspiration Influence* was demonstrated by my ability to inspire others to support my efforts in fighting against the establishment of a college system.

The unique combination of *Behavioral Influence*, *Rational Influence,* and *Emotional Influence* enabled me to come close to maximizing my influence on key members of the Princeton University administration. To this day, I am convinced that I played an important role in helping to temporarily delay the implementation of the Princeton University college system that has now been in place for almost 30 years. I am a very proud alumnus of Princeton which is still rated as the #1 university in the United States by respected magazines like *U.S. News & World Report*. Unfortunately, as anticipated, the residential college system eliminated hundreds of dining hall jobs for students. I, therefore, won the battle but lost the war. However, my experience as the CEO of the Commons Dining Halls of Princeton University was an excellent demonstration of the connection between leadership and *Intelligent Influence*.

Intelligent Influence Leadership Lessons

My experiences as the CEO of the Princeton University Commons mirrored those of leaders in every industry in the business world. There are four fundamental questions that leaders (regardless of the size of the organization that they lead) must answer in order to effectively utilize *Intelligent Influence* to achieve extraordinary success. These are the following:

1) What have been the most important influences in the life of the leader? (Influence Awareness)

This question helps leaders begin the process of understanding why they think the way they think and do what they do. It is also an important first step in assessing their personality type and skill set. This information will be essential in the *Influence Management* step of the *Intelligent Influence* process.

2) How is the leader currently influencing others in the context of the six types of Intelligent Influence? (Influence Impact)

It is essential that leaders understand their influence strengths and weaknesses so that they can develop an *Influence Management* plan that helps them achieve their specific goals.

3) What are the leader's External Influence goals and what Internal Influence investments are needed to make to achieve these goals? (Influence Management)

Once leaders understand their personality type, skill set, and *External Influence* goals, they will know what *Internal Influence* investments they need to make to be successful. The answer to this question provides them with a very clear road map to success.

4) What is the leader doing to have the Behavioral Influence (credibility), Rational Influence (creativity), and Emotional Influence (connection) that is necessary for extraordinary success? (Influence Maximization)

This question is never asked by average leaders. However, extraordinary leaders understand that they must demonstrate their *credibility* through *Behavioral Influence*; their *creativity* through *Rational Influence*; and their *connection* with the people they are attempting to influence through *Emotional Influence*. This strategic use of influence is the key to exceptional leadership success in any organization of any size.

CHAPTER 9

Sales: Chevrolet

The World's Greatest Salesman

Joe Girard has been considered by many to be the "World's Greatest Salesman" because of his record-breaking sales accomplishments. His incredible achievements include:

➢ Being named by the *Guiness Book of World Records* as the "World's Greatest Salesman" a record 12 times.

➢ Selling more retail "Big Ticket" items "one-at-a-time" than any other salesperson in any retail industry including houses, boats, motor homes, insurance, automobiles, etc.

➢ Averaging six new retail car or truck sales a day (no used automobiles or trucks).

➢ Selling 18 retail cars and trucks in one day (the most ever).

➢ Selling 174 retail cars and trucks in one month (the most ever).

➢ Selling 1,425 retail cars and trucks in one year (the most ever).

➤ Selling 13,001 retail cars and trucks at a Chevrolet dealership between 1963 and 1978 (the most ever for a 15-year career).

➤ Being inducted into the Automotive Hall of Fame.

Joe Girard, as he is known today, was born Joseph Samuel Gerard on November 1, 1928. He grew up in a very poor section of Detroit, Michigan, to immigrants from Italy struggling to survive in their new homeland. Joe did not know it at the time; however, his incredible path to sales success followed the same steps outlined by the *Intelligent Influence Framework*:

Intelligent Influence Framework™

	Internal Influence	External Influence
Influence Understanding	*Step 1* **Influence Awareness**	*Step 2* **Influence Impact**
Influence Actions	*Step 3* **Influence Management**	*Step 4* **Influence Maximization**

Influence Awareness

Joe's first step in the process of becoming a legendary salesman was exploring the important influences in his life. The foundation of his success was his willingness to go through the painful process of becoming *Influence Aware*. Unlike many sales professionals, he understood that recognizing the ways in which he had been influenced in his life was the first step in becoming the best salesperson he could be. Joe often said: "Look back to learn how to look forward better." After deep and difficult self-reflection, Joe identified three major influences (or as he calls them "sparks") that played a significant role in influencing him to pursue a path to extraordinary sales success.

The first major influence in his life was the unconditional love that he received from his mother Grace. She openly expressed her belief that Joe could be a success in whatever he chose to do. His mother told him continually that he could be an extraordinary success if he believed in himself and could effectively sell himself to others. Grace, therefore, played the most significant role in his early development because she was the first person to influence him to truly believe in his abilities.

The second major influence in his early life was his father. Joe Girard's father, Antonino Gerard, was an immigrant from Sicily who was emotionally and physically abusive to Joe. Joe felt that the lack of career success that his father found in America influenced him to continually put his son down. His dad was a negative influence who constantly berated him and told him that he would never be successful. However, his dad's negative influence became a positive motivator by influencing Joe to work as hard as he could to prove that his father's negative view of him was wrong. He spent much of his life attempting to show the world that his mother's belief in him was right and his father's views of him were completely inaccurate.

The third major influence in his early life was the boxer Joe Louis, who grew up in a section of Detroit that was not far from Joe Girard's boyhood home. Louis was the world heavyweight boxing champion from June 1937 to March 1949. Even though Joe Girard may have been a young white boy in a racially segregated country and Joe Louis was a black man, the white Joe admired the black Joe more than any other celebrity at the time.

Louis was the third major influence in Joe's life because he was also named Joe; grew up in virtually the same Detroit neighborhood; overcame tremendous barriers to become the best boxer in the world; and was the champion during Joe Girard's formative years (ages 8 to 20). Girard was convinced that if a black man from Detroit could be the best in the world, then he could be the best at what he wanted to be. Joe, therefore, followed Louis's career closely. Every one of the boxer's many victories served as a source of inspiration for Joe. Girard's focus on *Influence Awareness* served as the cornerstone of his success.

Influence Impact

One of the most frustrating things about positive influence is that it is not always immediate. It sometimes takes many years for a positive influence to take hold and guide someone to success. Unfortunately, negative influence is much more immediate. As naturally insecure human beings, we frequently allow negative comments and thoughts to limit us. This was true in Joe's youth. The negative influence of Joe's father took a toll on Joe. He never had confidence in his intellectual abilities, largely because of the criticism of his father. He, therefore, dropped out of high school and spent his youth doing odd jobs.

As a teenager, he learned how to make money but he could not find a career that he was passionate about. Joe worked as a shoeshine boy, a newspaper salesman, a dishwasher, a delivery boy, and a stove assembler. He enjoyed making money and worked very hard, but was never satisfied with his job or his pay. He was driven to pull himself out of poverty and become a business success to prove that his father was wrong and his mother was right about him. Joe became a fairly successful homebuilder for 13 years. However, in spite of his success, he never received praise from his father. As Joe has frequently said in interviews "not once did my father say he was proud of me."

Unfortunately, Joe's real estate business failed and, at the age of 35, he began the *Influence Impact* process by asking himself if he had the kind of professional influence that he wanted to have at this stage in his life. He may not have known about the six types of *Intelligent Influence*. However, Joe, like every other person who becomes an extraordinary success, examined his influence strengths and weaknesses. It is clear that Joe was not happy with the level of *Authority, Resource, Reputation, Thought, Belief and Inspiration Influences* that he had in his life at the time. He, therefore, felt compelled to pursue a brand new career that would enable him to have the kind of *Influence Impact* that he desired.

Influence Management

Joe was a hard worker with an insatiable drive to succeed. However, his previous jobs did not provide the level of reward he felt he deserved for his hard work. He was in debt, desperate for work, and convinced that the only profession that provided a direct reward for hard work was sales. Joe, therefore, dedicated himself to "getting into the sales game" as he called it. Unfortunately, he had a stuttering problem that prevented him from communicating as effectively as he wanted to with others. He knew that he would have to overcome his stuttering problem to become a successful salesman. He, therefore, initiated the process of *Influence Management* in preparation for a career in sales. He did not know it at the time, but he began this process by using the *Individual Influence Management* formula below:

Individual Influence Management

Personality Type (P) + Skills (S) + Internal Influence (I) = External Influence (E)

Where the symbols represent the following:

P = *The personality type of an individual.*

S = *The skills and abilities a person possesses.*

I = *The developmental influence action (training, coaching, team building, etc.).*

E = *The ways in which this person influences others as a result of actions.*

Girard intuitively knew that his personality and skills, at the time, could only take him so far in life. He, therefore, focused on getting the *Internal Influence* (as described in the box above) into his life that would enable him to get the most out of his personality and skills. This strategy, which is common to all extraordinarily successful people, was the secret behind his sales success.

Joe felt that hard work was the key to success in any endeavor. However, by going through some very difficult financial problems, he learned that the foundation of success is an intense "want." Joe knew that, no matter what a person wants to accomplish, that person will never achieve something significant unless he or she wants it bad enough to do whatever it takes to reach his or her goals. The challenges in his life taught him that the more a salesperson wants, the more he can achieve. In his speeches, he frequently states: "Knowing what you want will power your drive."

Girard was desperate for money and recognized that sales could be a way for him to feed his family. He, therefore, had the "want." Joe knew that he needed help to overcome his stuttering to succeed in sales. He had never heard of the term *Influence Management*. However, he desperately needed to succeed in sales to pay his bills. Girard, therefore, worked as hard as he possibly could to bring the influences into his life necessary to conquer his stuttering problem and become a successful salesman.

Joe read many different "How To" books and tried every trick available to address his speech limitations. His *Internal Influence* strategy of research, mental exercises, practice, and effective therapy paid off. Joe overcame his stuttering problem and, at the age of 35 with his enhanced communication skills, got a job as a Chevrolet car salesman in Detroit. He sold a car on his very first day and in just two months, because he was hungry and aggressive, became a top car salesman at the dealership. However, the other salesman saw his success as a threat to their livelihood and convinced the manager to fire him because he was "too aggressive."

This firing was a blessing in disguise because it enabled Joe to find a job at the dealership where he became a sales legend. He joined Merollis Chevrolet in Eastpointe, Michigan, in 1963 and stayed there until he retired in 1977. It was in this job that he set his amazing sales records. However, the *Influence Management* strategy that he utilized to overcome stuttering became the most valuable tool in his sales "tool-kit."

Joe felt comfortable enough at the dealership to strategically manage the influences in his life to become a successful salesman. He was a perpetual learner who bought many books on sales, leadership, and extraordinary achievement that were written by people who had a track record of success. He had little respect for business authors that were not successful business people. Joe worked day and night on perfecting the best sales, leadership, and human interaction techniques that he found in his research.

One of the most valuable lessons that he learned, through his quest for the most effective *Internal Influence*, was the power of positive thinking and influence. He was convinced that the negative outlook that most people have was not only reinforced by negative people, it was the key factor limiting their success.

Joe often tells the story of a golfer who, before an important putt, thinks to himself how difficult the putt is and misses the cup because he focused on the potential failure. He calls this presumption of failure "prequalifying." The successful golfer, like the successful salesperson, sees a challenge and, instead of prequalifying, says to himself: "Since I have accomplished this putt (or sales goal) before, I can do it now."

The most important lesson that Joe learned in life is that this positive outlook is intensified by surrounding oneself with positive people. He was convinced that the influence of positive people, on a regular basis, was the key to attaining extraordinary success. Likewise, the influence of negative people is the formula for failure. Joe likes to say, "If you hang around a garbage can long enough, you will stink." The negative influence of his father played an important role in motivating Joe to spend as little time as possible with negative people and negative news.

Joe learned that, by strategically managing the positive influences in his life, he was motivated to do things that few people thought were possible. These influences intensified his belief in himself and motivated him to focus on sales success so badly that he could taste it. He discovered that if you want to climb a mountain, focus on the top. The positive influences in his life enabled him to put blinders on (to block out negativity) and dedicate himself completely to achieving extraordinary sales success. Joe's strategy enabled him to do what few sales people have ever done—achieve *Influence Maximization* on a regular basis.

Influence Maximization

Joe liked to tell the story of how his mom "would sell me and say don't listen to him [referring to his dad]. I will never forget that one day she took me to a window and told me that there was something out there for everyone and that I needed to go out and find it and show him he is wrong." Girard found that "thing" and became the "World's Greatest Salesman" by maximizing the influence he had on his customers.

Joe learned early in life that sales people are not born; they are made. He often said, "Nobody is going to do nothing for you. You are the captain of your ship." Most people fail because Joe believed that they are "ATANA. All Talk And No Action." In contrast, Joe motivated himself by saying repeatedly: "If it's to be, it's up to me." He used this catchy mantra several times a day to motivate him, force him to be disciplined, avoid wasting time, and leave his house every day with a plan that he prepared the night before.

This strategy paid off in a record fashion. Most car salespeople sell approximately seven cars a month. Joe averaged six cars a day. His amazing success in closing deals with customers can be explained by the strategic way he utilized *The Caldwell Spheres of Influence* to achieve *Influence Maximization* which, as depicted in the recurring diagram on the next page, is the seamless integration of *Behavioral Influence, Rational Influence, and Emotional Influence.*

Caldwell Spheres of Influence

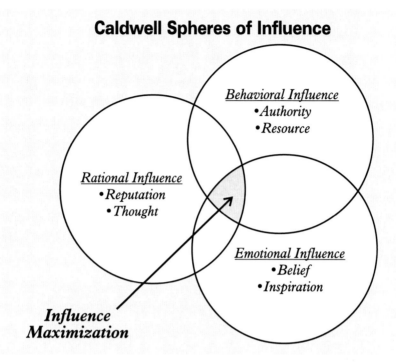

Behavioral Influence
• *Authority*
• *Resource*

Rational Influence
• *Reputation*
• *Thought*

Emotional Influence
• *Belief*
• *Inspiration*

Influence Maximization

Behavioral Influence

Joe's initial focus with potential customers was in establishing his sphere of *Behavioral Influence.* Joe frequently says that the process of learning to overcome stuttering was one of the best training experiences of his life because it forced him to think about what he wanted to say and (more importantly) what other people wanted to hear.

He became a better listener and was more adept at structuring exactly what he wanted to say to get the *credibility* he needed to influence his potential customers to recognize his *Authority Influence* and *Resource Influence.* The first step in developing the *credibility* that comes from *Behavioral Influence* is understanding the customer. Joe studied customers and learned that most consumers, whether they are buying groceries, cars, or advisory services, are a little scared. However, the simple fact that they take the time to come to a dealership, store, or meet with a professional advisor indicates that they need or want what is being offered.

Joe was convinced that there is an unspoken inherent distrust between salespeople and customers. Salespeople think that most customers are wasting their time while customers think most salespeople are focused on ripping them off. However, the goal of the sale is to turn this contentious relationship into a win-win partnership where both the customer and the salesperson get what they want and need.

Long before the Internet Age (where many people have more than 500 friends on the latest social media networking platform), Joe discovered the importance of social networks and referrals. He understood that if you treat someone very well, he or she would say good things about you to hundreds of other people. Likewise, if you treat someone poorly, many bad things would be said about you to other people.

The foundation of Joe's *Behavioral Influence* with his customers came from the *credibility* that he got from the people who referred him to friends and family. An extremely high percentage of Joe's sales came from referrals of one type or another. The foundation of his referral network and the source of his *credibility* were the people he called "birddogs" (because they helped him identify potential customers who were ready to buy a car).

Early on in his sales career, Joe understood the relatively simple premise that many sales people miss: the more referrals you get, the more sales you will make. He, therefore, offered as many people (the birddogs) as he could the chance to make $25 (which was a lot of money at the time) for referring someone who purchased a car from Joe. If a person who bought a car from Joe presented a Joe Girard business card with the name of a birddog on the back, Joe would send or give the birddog who made the referral $25.

This very simple sales referral trick was extremely effective because it used a combination of both *Resource Influence* and *Authority Influence* to generate *credibility* for Joe (even when he was not around). His birddogs included people who had bought a car from him—barbers, mechanics, bankers, insurance agents, family, and friends. He recruited anyone who had *credibility* with groups of people (friends, relatives, customers, etc.) who might be thinking about buying a car. By offering to pay others for referrals, Joe created a massive team of sales assistants who were receiving a commission to convince their customers, friends, and family that if they wanted a car, they had to go to Joe first.

His birddogs were influenced to believe that Joe was extraordinarily successful because of his willingness to share his financial *resources* with others. He, therefore, benefited from *Resource Influence*. His willingness to share financial *resources* influenced the birddogs to tell their customers, friends, and family that this successful person was the one *authority* on cars that they had to see if they were looking for the best car for their money.

Joe understood that *Authority Influence* was transferable from one person to another. Since many of these people were considered to be "authorities" in their own right (as mechanics, barbers, etc.), they transferred their *Authority Influence* to Joe every time they recommended him. Girard, therefore, had an amazing sphere of *Behavioral Influence* that motivated thousands of customers to consider him to be *credible*. However, that was not enough to close the sale.

Rational Influence

Joe understood that establishing *credibility* with potential customers was just the start. His success was enhanced significantly because of his willingness to do *creative* things to get customers into the showroom. He benefited from developing a sphere of *Rational Influence* which is comprised of *Reputation Influence* and *Thought Influence*.

Girard also knew the value of a business card in the process of influencing customers to buy cars. He went out of his way to use this important marketing tool in unique ways. Since everyone who could drive a car was a potential customer, he would hand out his business cards whenever and wherever he could.

When Joe was eating a meal at a restaurant, he would be very friendly to waiters or waitresses and leave a big tip and his business card so that they would remember him the next time they needed a car. He would bring bags of cards to sporting events and "accidentally" throw them out when everyone was standing during an exciting play.

His strategic sharing of his business cards helped to provide valuable *Reputation Influence*. Girard's legend grew because of his success as a salesman and the *creative* and liberal ways in which he would share his business cards with people in the community around Merollis Chevrolet. His business cards were talked about so much that they became famous and helped to increase the demand to buy cars from Joe. Girard used his good reputation to build an even better reputation by letting everyone know who he was, what he did, and that he was the best at doing it.

Joe was so concerned about his reputation that he personally hired Deloitte & Touche (currently the largest auditing firm in the world) when he was the top car salesperson in the country to verify that each sale was one at a time. He wanted the world to know that his car sales were not the result of large companies buying lots of cars from him. Instead, his sales were generated the same way that the average car salesman generates sales . . . one car at a time. This fact makes his accomplishments that much more impressive.

Girard never finished high school, but was brilliant when it came to developing a sales marketing plan. His prospecting activity was guided by his meticulously organized index card system. Joe developed two sets of index cards of past and potential customer files. The first set was an alphabetical listing of old and potentially new customers, so he could find anyone if he knew the last name. The second set was in date order, so he knew when he needed to contact people to schedule a time to meet with them at the dealership.

Joe was one of the first individual salesmen to get potential customers to read his mailings by sending 12 pieces of mail (one a month) in different color and shape envelopes to his contacts each year. The uniqueness of his mailing campaigns helped him develop *Thought Influence* in the minds of his potential customers. During his free time at the dealership, Girard would work on mailings to get his business card out while he waited for his turn at the customers. The envelopes contained a note with a simple timely message (January's included "Happy New Year!" February's "Happy Valentine's Day!" etc.) ending with "I Like You, from Joe Girard, Merollis Chevrolet."

The uniquely *creative* way that Joe used referrals, distributed business cards, and sent mailings provided the *Reputation Influence* and *Thought Influence* that he needed to convince many potential customers that he was the kind of personable and innovative salesman that they should buy a car from. He was, without question, the most talked-about car salesman in each of his target households.

Joe understood the importance of having a reputation as a car salesman who gives his customers extraordinary deals. He, therefore, spent considerable time cultivating his image. Girard knew that the foundation of a successful reputation is being extremely organized. Joe, therefore, structured each day to make the most positive impression he could on as many people as possible. He avoided wasting time while he was on the job. Joe spent very little time "hanging out" with other salespeople because he had a laser focus on selling as many cars as he could every work day to make as much money as possible.

Before going to bed the night before, he developed a list of things that he needed to do the next day. Therefore, the first thing Joe did when he got to the dealership was review what he had to do that day. He went over his appointments and identified the sales calls he needed to make from his elaborate index-card marketing system. Girard recognized that his plans would change frequently during the day. However, by planning his day and working his plan, he found that he was better prepared for that first sale of the day that, if it happened early, would provide the influence necessary to catapult him to many additional sales throughout the day.

People underestimate the power of *Influence-Driven Momentum*^{TM}. It is amazing how often sports teams get hot, at the right time, and find themselves in a winning streak that propels them to the championship. Sportscasters often say that the team's momentum made them unstoppable. In fact, if you think about it, it is rare when a team that does not have momentum wins a championship. Webster's dictionary defines the word *momentum* as *"the strength or force gained by motion or series of events." Influence-Driven Momentum* is defined as *"the process of an immediate past success providing sufficient influence on a person or group of people to propel them to even greater present success."*

This critical aspect of influence is a key part of the strategy of many sports teams. However, it has been largely ignored in business. *Influence-Driven Momentum* is the secret of success of exceptional salespeople. They understand that they are more likely to get a new sale shortly after their previous sale because of the confidence, energy, and positive outlook derived from that sale. They strategically use this influence by filling their pipeline of sales so that they have a higher probability of finding someone willing to buy shortly after they closed a previous sale. This second sale would lead to a third sale which would lead to many more sales.

Joe was a master at the strategic use of sales momentum. By focusing on a sale early in the day, he was able to build on this sale to generate on average five more sales that day. He, therefore, was able to average six sales a day when most car salespeople only average seven sales a month. He may not have known it at the time; however, Joe's use of *Influence-Driven Momentum* was one of the major reasons that he sold more cars on a daily basis than any other car salesperson in history. Girard, therefore, had an amazing sphere of *Rational Influence* that motivated customers to consider him to be *creative*.

Emotional Influence

Joe was able to establish his *credibility* with many clients through his frequent referral network. He was able to demonstrate his *creativity* with potential clients through the uniqueness of his sales approach. A lot of very good salesmen and women can do those things. However, most salespeople do not work on enhancing their *Emotional Influence*. Joe was extraordinary because he was able to develop an emotional *connection* with prospects and each of the people who bought a car from him.

Girard's powerful *connection* with people was developed through his hard work and extraordinary commitment to record keeping. Joe went out of his way to capture personal information on every person that he spoke with. Whether or not a person was ready to buy a car, he wanted to know a potential customer's birthday, the names of their children, favorite sports teams, dream vacation spots, the best meal they ever had, etc.

He recorded this information on index cards that he filed in a system that would allow him to find the information whenever he wanted to contact a particular person. Joe knew the importance of connecting with the emotional needs of each potential customer. Most people are in a positive mood and feel good when they think about their children, birthday, favorite food, or vacation spot. Joe made a special effort to use this valuable information to *connect* his name with the positive feelings of potential customers.

Simple things like sending a personalized birthday card on someone's birthday or sending a picture of their favorite vacation spot helped to *connect* Joe with the positive things in a potential customer's life. He effectively utilized *Belief Influence* by appealing to the common beliefs (a particular food, vacation, or restaurant was the best) of potential customers. Girard also utilized *Inspiration Influence* by inspiring people to think that purchasing a car can feel as good as an excellent meal or be as much fun as a fantastic vacation.

Instead of thinking of Joe as a typical car salesman who was like every other salesman (a necessary evil in purchasing a car), Joe was thought of as that considerate family friend who actually cared about your feelings and those things that were important to you. He, therefore, connected emotionally with people in a way that few salespeople can.

Joe's emotional connection with people convinced them to come to the dealership to see him when they needed a car. It did not close the sale. However, once he met with potential customers, he went out of his way to re-establish the emotional connection with his potential customers. He would demonstrate genuine joy in seeing them and, after reviewing their file of favorite things (prior to their arrival at the dealership), ask if they had recently gone to their favorite restaurant or dream vacation spot (both of which, to their amazement, he would name).

Most salespeople focus exclusively on selling a product when they are with a customer. They don't care about a person's life outside of their need for the product they are trying to sell. These unenlightened salespeople, therefore, lose a lot of sales because they have not formed the emotional connection that most prospects need to be convinced to give a particular salesperson their money.

Joe was different because he effectively used positive comments to put people at ease. He would compliment a person's clothes, their eyeglasses, or their children. Girard's elaborate record-keeping system gave him personalized insights that other salespersons would not have. Joe could ask about someone's birthday last week or how their daughter is enjoying a particular school or if they had played their favorite sport recently. He was focused on connecting with customers emotionally by ensuring that they liked, trusted, confided, and believed in Joe's ability to sell them a quality car at a fair price.

Joe was also unique in that he had a passionate interest in his *Influence Impact* on every customer. He wanted to know how he successfully or unsuccessfully influenced others so that he could increase his sales in the future. At the end of each day, Girard would assess his *Influence Impact* by replaying the day in his mind to reflect on what he did right and what he didn't do right to have the *Emotional Influence* he needed to make a sale.

Joe felt that nothing was more important than understanding how a customer's feeling about the sales interaction differed from the feelings of the salesperson. Success in the sales process comes from narrowing the *Emotional Influence* gap between the salesperson and the customer. A sale is made when there is no gap between the two people.

At the end of each day, Joe, therefore, reviewed what he said or did to make a person buy. He also thought about the mistakes that he made during the day. Girard often called people who did not buy from him and asked them for feedback on what he did wrong and what he could have done more effectively (to influence them to buy). Amazingly, these lost prospects would often tell him the honest truth (how they felt he came on too strong, why they desired a different make of car, that they were just looking, or how they felt they could get a better price elsewhere). Joe focused on improving every day. His commitment to excellence enabled him to have an amazing sphere of *Emotional Influence*. Joe's incredible mastery of this sphere motivated customers to develop the emotional connection necessary to influence them to buy a car from him.

Intelligent Influence Sales Lessons

Joe Girard's extraordinary sales success provides a powerful road map for those who consider themselves to be sales professionals. His willingness to undertake the sometimes painful process of *Influence Awareness* (by examining the positive and negative influences in his life) provided the foundation he needed to begin to build a career in sales. Joe's honest assessment of his *Influence Impact* helped him understand his developmental needs (overcome stuttering, learning the sales and car businesses, etc.).

Girard's willingness to study his successes and failures and continually improve on his sales skills every day provided him with the *Influence Management* he needed to become a top car salesman in his region. However, his ability to utilize *Behavioral Influence, Rational Influence, and Emotional Influence* made him the "World's Greatest Salesperson."

There are four fundamental questions that every sales professional must answer in order to achieve *Influence-Driven Sales*. These are the following:

1) What past and present influences are affecting my interest, ability, and drive to be a salesperson? (Influence Awareness)

2) How am I currently influencing or not influencing potential customers? (Influence Impact)

3) What Internal Influences do I need to become a more effective and successful salesperson? (Influence Management)

4) How do I develop a personal sales process that will enable me to have the Behavioral Influence, Rational Influence, and Emotional Influence that will influence large numbers of people to buy my product or service over those of my competitors? (Influence Maximization)

The sales professionals who strategically follow a sales plan, built around the answers to these important questions, will be able to achieve the extraordinary success that comes from utilizing *Intelligent Influence* in the sales process.

CHAPTER 10
Diversity: Deloitte

The Rule, Not the Exception

I end this section of the book with a chapter on a subject that has given me my greatest highs and lows in the business world. Diversity and inclusion are often thought as being the least important focus of a business because many executives naively think that it does not directly affect the bottom line of a company. However, in today's complex business world, the opposite is true.

Diversity used to be the exception, not the rule. In yesterday's business world, people with almost identical backgrounds and perspectives dominated virtually every key position in large companies. However, today there are four generations in the workplace, significantly more women and minorities in every profession, and a global workforce of white and brown people who think very differently than the leaders of the businesses world of just a few years ago. Most importantly, the customer base of most companies is even more diverse than the new global workforce.

Diversity is now the rule, not the exception. Companies that can manage this 21st century workforce in a way that enables them to effectively market to a diverse customer base will be extraordinarily successful. Companies that are unwilling to embrace diversity are guaranteed to fail over the long run. Consequently, managing diversity and inclusion is the single most important factor in business profitability and productivity.

This was not always the case. When I graduated from Princeton in 1982 and joined the Quaker Oats Company in Shiremanstown, Pennsylvania, as a production supervisor, I realized how little attention Fortune 500 companies paid to leveraging diversity to increase profitability. These companies were able to get away with a monolithic workforce because businesses in the United States did not have as much global competition and need for price compression as they do today. A big company could be very successful, even if it did not have the best employees. Companies could hire and fire people, at will, without any significant impact on the bottom line. However, in today's world, where companies are focused on quarterly profitability in a global marketplace, it is essential that companies hire the best employees, regardless of how old they are or what they look like. A company that discriminates is virtually guaranteed to lose market share in the competitive business world of today.

Discrimination in My First Job

Unfortunately, things were different in 1982. My success managing the Commons Dining Halls made me an attractive candidate for the Quaker Oats management development program which identified future plant managers and executives. I decided to take the Quaker Oats job offer over one that I received from Arthur Anderson in New York largely because the salary was 25% higher at Quaker. However, I was shocked when I arrived at the plant. There were three very surprising things about this new position that horrified me. First, the person with the least seniority in the plant had been there 15 years. It was clear that new employees were second-class citizens and longevity was valued more than productivity. I, therefore, had an uphill battle simply because I was a new employee.

Second, there was not one African-American or Latino person in any position anywhere in the plant. It became very clear that I was the only person with brown skin who had ever worked at the plant. It was much more difficult than I imagined, being the only person of color in the plant. It felt like I was constantly being scrutinized because I was different. This challenge was compounded because I lived in an area where very few African-American or Latino people lived at the time. It seems funny today; however, I found myself regularly watching reruns of the television show *The Jeffersons* in my apartment to have the comfort of seeing successful black people.

Finally and most disturbing of all, my supervisor was a high school graduate who never attended college and seemed to have a chip on his shoulder because he had to manage this black kid who had just graduated from Princeton. I was a naïve recent college grad who had no idea that I had absolutely no chance of succeeding in this position. I was able to effectively manage the production team that I supervised. In fact, I really enjoyed that part of the job. The people whom I supervised were fantastic and treated me with great respect. However, my boss fired me after ten months for no legitimate reason. Like many other people of color in this position, I was a devastated, insecure black kid who thought he was a failure and did not know what to do with his career.

Unfortunately, this story was commonplace to the business world of the 1980s. Companies could get away with firing people who simply did not "fit in" (code for not looking or acting like the long-term white employees). The business world was dominated largely by white American men who acted and thought in a very similar way. The vast majority of these leaders did not have a racist bone in their body; however, it was clear that all employees (whether they were white or black) had to fit in seamlessly with the culture or find another job. Unfortunately, many talented white and black people who had different influences in their life, prior to joining the firm, were fired because they were different, not because they were not talented. Firms, therefore, lost a lot of outstanding employees.

Today's business world is very different. Rapid technological advancements, combined with globalization, have made the integration of diversity the rule rather than the exception. Aviation innovations have led to easier global travel. In addition, current technology has provided amazing new opportunities for individuals who have been trained to understand the technical aspects of software and hardware development. The seamless interconnection of global economies has made international commerce an essential part of doing business.

Businesses are now being run by more and more people who were born outside of the United States. In addition, there are significantly more women, people of African descent, and Latinos at every level of corporations. This is complicated by the fact that there are four generations of employees with very different perspectives on work. The need for a more technical and financially competitive workforce has led to a rapid increase in the number of Indian, Japanese, and Chinese employees (who come from educational systems that influence students to develop an expertise in technology).

These cataclysmic changes in the business world have made the ability to manage people with diverse backgrounds and perspectives the single greatest leadership challenge in the 21st century. This new reality is the most significant reason why *Intelligent Influence Workshops*[TM] and *Intelligent Influence Executive Coaching*[TM] are rapidly becoming the development approaches of choice by large and small companies. This unique approach to leadership in the 21st century, because it is customized to each individual, is the most effective way to significantly increase the productivity of diverse employees in an organization of any size.

Finding Success at Deloitte

I was so ashamed of being fired from my first real job that I did not tell anyone about it and struggled for several months trying to find a job. However, the positive influence that my Princeton degree and leadership at Commons had on my self-confidence (and potential employers) enabled me to regain enough of a belief in myself to actively pursue a new career. If, like many young people of color, I had not been influenced to believe that I could succeed in a business world that was not welcoming of black and brown people I might have given up on pursuing a career as a senior executive in a major corporation.

If this had happened, then discrimination would have taken yet another victim in the business world. My success in other leadership positions later in my career indicated that, because of discrimination and intentional segregation, Quaker Oats likely lost a person of color that could have been a key leader in their organization. Companies could afford to do that then; however, in today's competitive environment, companies cannot afford to lose talented employees.

Fortunately, after passing the General Securities Representative Examination (better known as the Series 7 Stockbroker Test) on my own, I was able to get a job with Dean Witter and eventually become a Certified Financial Planner (CFP). My Princeton degree, Commons leadership experience, and new focus on personal finance helped me gain acceptance to the University of Pennsylvania Wharton School where I received a MBA in Finance in 1988. After graduation, I joined the management consulting firm Touche Ross which merged two years later with Deloitte, Haskins and Sells and formed a new company called Deloitte & Touche. I loved the firm and rose from the positions of associate consultant to consultant to manager to senior manager in five years.

I had two outstanding bosses and a senior human resources executive who sponsored me as I rose in the firm. Thanks to their support, I became the first black senior manager in the New York and New Jersey management consulting practice. In addition, thanks to a nomination from senior partners at Deloitte & Touche, I received the prestigious Harlem YMCA's "Black Achievers in Industry Award." I finally felt vindicated. My firing from Quaker Oats was a diversity low point in my life while becoming the first black senior manager in the Northeast Region of Deloitte was a diversity high point for me. Through this process, I learned a great deal about the hurdles that people of color face as they rise through the ranks and I felt an obligation (largely because my parents influenced me to always focus on helping others) to help people of color succeed in the business world.

Founding ABLE

I, therefore, used my influence as a new senior manager in 1993 to team with a dynamic administrative professional and good friend Tim Washington to voluntarily form an organization in Deloitte's Parsippany, New Jersey office called the "Association of Black and Latino Employees" (ABLE). This was the first organization in the firm that brought client service professionals together with administrative professionals to mentor each other and complete community service projects.

This organization was a phenomenal success in the minds of senior executives in the firm because Deloitte & Touche received a great deal of positive press for our community service projects. I was personally very proud of this group because, under my leadership, we increased minority employee performance and retention. However, the long-term value of this group came from our ability to convince partners that there was tangible value in programs focused on diversity and inclusion. ABLE was the first organization of its kind at the firm. I am proud to say that Deloitte is now one of the largest accounting and consulting firms in the world and has fully embraced employee affinity groups modeled after ABLE.

Founding the NABMC

I really enjoyed my work as a senior manager; however, I developed even more satisfaction from leading an organization like ABLE that was "able" to help so many employees. Even though my work at ABLE was time-consuming, I gained significantly more visibility and respect in the firm. I saw the incredible value of creating an affinity group within the firm and, when I realized how little diversity there was in the ranks of the world's largest management consulting firms, decided to form the first national inter-company affinity group in the management consulting profession. I formed an organization called the "National Association of Black Management Consultants, Inc." (NABMC) in 1995.

I discovered through my interactions with partners and senior managers in other consulting firms that, in the major management consulting firms in the world at the time (Anderson Consulting; A.T. Kearney; Bain & Co.; Booz Allen Hamilton; Boston Consulting Group; Coopers & Lybrand; Deloitte & Touche; Ernst & Young; KPMG; McKinsey & Co.; Price Waterhouse, etc.), there were only 11 black partners and 24 black senior managers. These numbers were horrifying, considering that there were thousands of white partners and senior managers in these firms alone. It was very clear that management consulting was one of the most influential and least diverse occupations in the world.

Unfortunately, at the time, many white business leaders did not understand the benefits of organizations that supported the development of a particular minority group. They thought that these groups were an unproductive way of self-segregation that increased the likelihood of the failure of minorities in the profession. The unspoken view of many of these leaders was that the only way to succeed in the firm was to simply adapt to the organization's culture and do exactly what everyone else does. However, these leaders lacked *Influence Awareness* and were not able to comprehend the reality that the influences in the lives of most of the minority recruits were so different than the influences in the lives of the partners that they could not fit into the organization without significant developmental support provided by organizations like ABLE or the NABMC. If these individuals (most of whom were as talented and intelligent as anyone in their respective firms) did not receive this type of influence, they were guaranteed to fail. The consulting firms would, therefore, lose talented individuals and waste millions of dollars in training.

Deloitte was unique in that (because of the success of ABLE) they understood my leadership ability and the inherent value of the NABMC. Senior management believed that the organization could be very helpful in their efforts to recruit talented minority consultants. I was still serving actively in my role as a senior manager. However, the firm (to their credit) allowed me to volunteer my time (as long as it did not interfere with my client work) to establish the NABMC. I am proud to say that this small organization that I founded in 1995 was extremely effective in helping the major management consulting firms recruit, train, and develop talented minority consultants. I did not know it at the time, however, ABLE and the NABMC were successful because they followed the steps outlined in the *Intelligent Influence* process as shown in the framework diagram on the next page:

Intelligent Influence Framework™

	Internal Influence	External Influence
Influence Understanding	Step 1 **Influence Awareness**	Step 2 **Influence Impact**
Influence Actions	Step 3 **Influence Management**	Step 4 **Influence Maximization**

Influence Awareness

As one of the few people of African descent at Deloitte & Touche, I learned early in my career how to examine in detail the large differences in the influences in my life and the influences in the lives of the white men and women with whom I worked. I had the opportunity to work with some fantastic people. However, even though I went to a predominantly white school like Princeton, my worldview and their worldview were very different. It was clear that the influences in their lives were closely aligned and the influences in my life were very, very different. The very first indication of this was my amazement at the frequency with which some of the senior executives would say negative things about each other behind their backs and still go out and have a drink or play a round of golf together on a regular basis.

I was the son of a minister and elementary school teacher who influenced me to have the mentality of a boy scout. I was influenced to believe that it was essential to treat people with respect whether or not they were present. It was not in my nature to bad-mouth people behind their backs and pretend to be their friend when I was with them. I did not change my style. However, I learned not to be bothered by this kind of duplicity in the workplace. I started to hone my *Influence Awareness* skills and developed a fascination with understanding why people do what they do and think the way they think. I did not know it at the time, but this was the beginning of my developing the concept of *Intelligent Influence*.

It became very clear to me that the more time people spend thinking about the influences in other people's lives, the better they become at understanding why people do what they do and think the way they think. This *Influence Awareness* skill has served me well throughout my life and was the main reason that I decided to start ABLE. I was disturbed to discover that the black and Latino client service professionals (the accountants, consultants, and tax professionals) and the black and Latino administrative professionals (secretaries and operational staff) did not seem to work together well.

The influence of "class" seemed to lead to a divide between these two groups, even though they were much more alike than different in the firm. The client service professionals had college or graduate school degrees and were new to the firm. They often had a self-confidence that could be misinterpreted as arrogance. Many of the administrative employees did not have college degrees and were somewhat insecure in their abilities. However, they had the advantage of experience because many of them had been with the firm for ten or more years. It became very clear to me that the only way that both groups could succeed in a firm, with so few people of color, was if they worked together.

I started the NABMC for similar reasons. After attending the National Black MBA Association Annual Conference for several years, I had a chance to interact with many of the most senior black management consulting professionals in the industry. Most of these amazing people were graduates of the best undergraduate and MBA programs in the world. These brilliant individuals often found it very difficult to succeed in their firms because the influences in their lives were very different that the influences in the lives of the older white partners that ran their respective firms. There was frequently a "culture clash" in the firms and very talented minorities were fired. It was clear that there was a need, for an outside organization, to help the leaders of the major management consulting firms and their minority employees work together more effectively. I therefore founded the NABMC and ran it with one of my best friends

Dexter Bridgeman. In hindsight it is clear that the NABMC was born out of my *Influence Awareness* of the management consulting profession.

Influence Impact at ABLE and the NABMC

The second step in the process of forming ABLE and the NABMC was *Influence Impact*. I did not know it at the time; however, I examined the influence of ABLE and the NABMC using the six types of *Intelligent Influence* as follows:

- *Authority Influence: ABLE* – As a new senior manager at Deloitte & Touche, I worked closely with the senior partners in the region to get their support for the establishment of ABLE. This gave the group the *Authority Influence* it needed to garner the active participation and support of key leaders in the firm.

- *Authority Influence: NABMC* – The NABMC was able to get *Authority Influence* very quickly by establishing an NABMC Annual Conference at the same time and in the same city as the National Black MBA Association Conference. First impressions are lasting. Our first conference gave us instant *credibility* because it was held at the Ritz-Carlton in Boston. In addition, we had 18% (2 of the 11) of the black management consulting partners in the world in attendance. Even though we were a volunteer-run organization, we hit the ground running.

- *Belief Influence: ABLE* – Since ABLE was the first organization of its kind at Deloitte, the employees were skeptical of its ability to succeed. However, our first event "Diversity Tastes Good" convinced employees to *believe* in the potential of ABLE to bring people together. At this first event, we highlighted the one type of diversity that people around the world are passionate about: food. We had employees of all races and backgrounds bring in food representing their heritage. The food was fantastic. More importantly, it served to provide ABLE with the *Belief Influence* it needed to convince employees and partners to *believe* in the potential of ABLE.

- *Belief Influence: NABMC* – The NABMC recruited volunteers to contact minority consultants in firms around the country to find out what their needs were. We also provided valuable career advice to consultants and recruitment advice to partners. This helped the NABMC create a powerful network that generated significant *Belief Influence* with the partners and employees of the major management consulting. We had convinced key people in the profession to *believe* in the potential of the NABMC.

- *Inspiration Influence: ABLE* – To bring client service and administrative professionals together, we focused ABLE's initial activities on helping urban students succeed in school. Most of the members of the organization grew up in urban communities and understood how difficult it was for students in these areas to succeed in school. We, therefore, developed some extremely inspirational programs providing needed mentoring to students. This generated an amazing amount of *Inspiration Influence* with ABLE members and Deloitte leaders. Everyone involved was *inspired* by these fantastic programs.

- *Inspiration Influence: NABMC* – The NABMC brought minority consultants from different firms together to discuss ways to overcome the challenges that they faced at work. Many of these discussions became very emotional as people explained their frustrations at work. This open and honest discussion, in a safe environment, helped the NABMC garner significant *Inspiration Influence* both in the minds of members and the leaders of the industry.

- *Reputation Influence: ABLE* – ABLE's *reputation* among members, employees, and partners grew exponentially when positive newspaper articles were written about Deloitte's fantastic efforts helping urban students. As news of these positive articles about Deloitte spread throughout the firm, ABLE's *Reputation Influence* grew.

- *Reputation Influence: NABMC* – As more and more partners and directors of human resources learned about the NABMC's positive efforts to increase the success of minority consultants, the *Reputation Influence* of the organization grew rapidly. I was, therefore, asked to present to formal and informal groups of minority consultants in major firms around the country.

- *Resource Influence: ABLE* – One of the most important lessons that I learned at ABLE was how easily administrative professionals could access needed *resources*. The client service professionals had the *Authority Influence* in the firm; however, the administrative professionals clearly had the *Resource Influence* needed to get things done.

- *Resource Influence: NABMC* – The NABMC was a volunteer organization that had limited financial resources. However, we were able to get the *resources* we needed from partners and senior managers who had *Resource Influence* in their respective firms.

- *Thought Influence: ABLE* – ABLE was a successful "affinity organization" (an employee group within a corporation that brings people together with like interests or backgrounds) largely because of the innovative internal mentoring programs that we developed. We spent considerable time teaching employees the secrets of success in a unique partnership like Deloitte & Touche. The program developed significant *Thought Influence* because we were able to create programs that had value for both client service and administrative professionals.

- *Thought Influence: NABMC* – The NABMC went out of its way to incorporate the new ideas of members. This enabled us to be the *thought* leader when it came to issues of diversity in the management consulting profession. My explanation of the difference between mentors and sponsors (which provided a lot of consultants with valuable insight into the secrets of success in the profession) helped to give the NABMC significant *Thought Influence* in the profession.

The review of ABLE and the NABMC's *Influence Impact* was extremely helpful in the development of the following *Influence Management* plans that laid the foundation for each organization's success.

Influence Management

To ensure the sustainable success of both ABLE and the NABMC, I intuitively initiated the *Influence Management* process as depicted in the table on the next page:

> ### Organization Influence Management
>
> *Organization Culture (O) + Capabilities (C) + Internal Influence (I) = External Influence (E)*
>
> Where the symbols represent the following:
>
> *O = The organization's culture.*
>
> *C = The capabilities of the organization (research, development, production, sales, etc.).*
>
> *I = The developmental influence action (acquisitions, alliances, consulting, divestitures, change in product offerings, partnerships, etc.).*
>
> *E = The ways in which the organization influences others as a result of the organization's actions.*

Influence Management at ABLE

At the time that we started ABLE, the *culture* of Deloitte and Touche was still evolving. Deloitte, Haskins and Sells was an audit-and-accounting-driven firm that was much more conservative than the more aggressive consulting-driven Touche Ross. One of the goals of ABLE was to help integrate members into a developing Deloitte & Touche culture that valued time management, cost control, and strong communication skills.

However, the culture of ABLE, as an organization as well as the collective skill set of the members, was bifurcated. Half of ABLE was comprised of administrative professionals who rarely traveled but were extremely organized and maintained close control of their schedule. The other half of ABLE were client service professionals who traveled all the time, lived chaotic lives, and had little or no control of their schedule. These differences were magnified because the client service professionals made significantly more than the administrative professionals who had been with the company a much longer time.

I recognized that there were some critical *Internal Influences* that I needed to initiate to begin to accomplish the two primary *External Influence* goals of ABLE. The first of these *External Influence* goals was to figure out a way to get the client service and administrative members of ABLE to work together and succeed in the firm. The second of these goals was to establish ABLE as an organization that was valuable to the firm. I recognized that community service projects could potentially provide the *Internal Influences* necessary to achieve the *External Influence* goals of bringing ABLE members together and getting the firm's support by getting articles written about Deloitte's great work on these projects.

One of my favorite things to do in life is to create innovative new programs that help young people. I utilized this skill to develop several programs that were incubated by ABLE. This included "Take Your Community To Work Day" where urban students spend a day at Deloitte; "Classroom Press Conference" where successful role models visit students in multiple classrooms; and the "Student Co-op Program" where students participated in month-long, summer accounting internships. Each of these programs was extraordinarily successful in teaching urban students about career opportunities and connecting them with mentors. They also established Deloitte as a leader in their industry in community service in New Jersey and New York. These successful programs provided the *Internal Influences* I had hoped for to achieve the *External Influence* goals of bringing client service and administrative professionals together; helping them succeed; and enabling ABLE to get the respect and support of leaders in the firm.

Influence Management at NABMC

Since the NABMC was an independent nonprofit volunteer organization, the culture was driven by social entrepreneurship. Those involved had an intense full-time management consulting job, so the time that they contributed to the organization took away from their free time; however, everyone involved had a passion for helping others. In addition, these people were among the smartest young people in the business world. The profile of the typical management consultant was someone who had done extremely well as an undergraduate student and completed one of the top five MBA programs in the world. As a result, the NABMC volunteers were a very highly skilled and intelligent group of people.

The NABMC had two primary *External Influence* goals. The first of these goals was to establish itself as the leading association for minority management consultants. The second of these goals was to provide valuable information about the secret of success of minorities in the management consulting profession. We utilized the culture and skills of the NABMC family to accomplish these goals in two very effective ways.

First, we established a conference featuring some of the most successful minority management consultants in the world. We held this conference just before and in the same location as the National Black MBA Association Conference to ensure that our programs were well attended. These conferences were held in exclusive hotels in Anaheim, Atlanta, Boston, Detroit, and New Orleans. These successful conferences had the *External Influence* effect that we planned. Consultants, from around the world, began to recognize the NABMC as the leading minority organization in the management consulting profession.

Second, we recognized that a small percentage of the people that needed our services could attend our annual conference. I, therefore, teamed up with Dexter Bridgeman, who happened to be an extraordinary publisher, and created *Management Consulting Magazine*. This unique publication was the first in the profession and featured unique insights into the secret of success of partners and senior managers in management consulting. The magazine was targeted to minority management consultants. It was extremely well received and provided the *External Influence* we desired. The tipping point came when we featured the first woman managing partner of Bain & Co. on the cover. The magazine helped us accomplish both of our goals. We had achieved the visibility we desired in the industry while, at the same time, providing the valuable information that minority consultants needed to succeed.

Influence Maximization

ABLE and the NABMC's successful use of *Influence Awareness*, *Influence Impact*, and *Influence Management* enabled them to break new ground and excel in their efforts to help diverse employees succeed in the very competitive and intense accounting and management consulting professions. These organizations were able to excel because of their

effective use of the fourth step in the *Intelligent Influence* process—
Influence Maximization. The process of maximizing influence is depicted
in the diagram below:

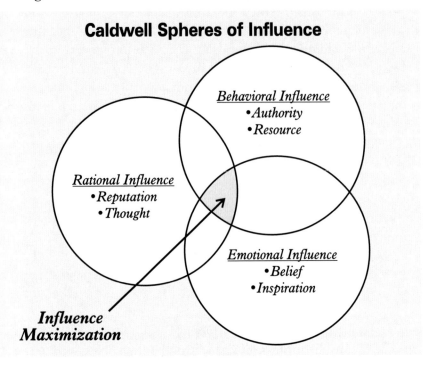

Caldwell Spheres of Influence

ABLE and the NABMC utilized *Behavioral Influence* to establish
themselves as an authority in their area of expertise with the resources
to accomplish their goals. They utilized *Rational Influence* by developing a
solid reputation as innovators helping minorities succeed at work. Finally,
they utilized *Emotional Influence* by getting members to believe in the
value of the organization and inspiring them to take advantage of the
programs these organizations offered. The foundation of the extraordinary
success of ABLE and the NABMC was the way that the leadership team
of these organizations utilized *Intelligent Influence* to significantly increase
the probability of success of minorities in professional service firms.

Intelligent Influence Diversity Lessons

Since diversity is now the rule and not the exception in the business
world, this book has focused on helping leaders utilize the *Intelligent*

Influence process to effectively manage diverse groups of people in any environment in any industry. In this sectionof the book, I provide advice for those people who feel like they are a member of a minority group in their organization. I use the term "minority" to apply to anyone who feels excluded from the current culture of the organization or office where they work. The key to effective diversity and inclusion is helping each "minority" employee identify one or more sponsors (the person or the groups of people responsible for determining whether or not they get promoted, a raise, or fired). Without a sponsor, people who look or feel different (regardless of the quality of their work) are guaranteed to fail. There are four fundamental questions that every minority must answer in order to effectively utilize *Intelligent Influence* to achieve extraordinary success. These questions, from the perspective of the minority employee, are:

1) What have been the most important influences in my life and the life of the sponsor that I am attempting to influence? (Influence Awareness)

This question helps minorities begin the process of understanding why they think the way they think and do what they do. It is also an important first step in assessing their personality type and skill set. Most importantly, it helps them begin to understand how to positively influence their sponsor or potential sponsor.

2) How am I currently influencing my sponsor and the people I work with in the context of the six types of Intelligent Influence? (Influence Impact)

It is essential that minorities understand their influence strengths and weaknesses so that they can develop an *Influence Management* plan that helps them achieve their specific goals.

3) What are my External Influence goals and what Internal Influence investments do I need to make to achieve these goals? (Influence Management)

Once a minority understands his or her personality type, skill set, and *External Influence* goals, he or she will know what *Internal Influence* investments are necessary to be successful. The answer to this question provides a very clear road map of ways to strategically influence the sponsor.

4) What am I doing to have the Behavioral Influence (credibility); Rational Influence (creativity); and Emotional Influence (connection) necessary for extraordinary success? (Influence Maximization)

The most interesting finding of both ABLE and the NABMC was the way that minority employees can use the *Caldwell Spheres of Influence* to succeed. It is essential that those, hoping to succeed in an organization where they are a minority, must have *Behavioral Influence, Rational Influence,* and *Emotional Influence* with their sponsors. *Behavioral Influence* is the ability to influence people to DO things based on the *credibility* of the individual. For anyone, especially minorities, it is essential that they are considered to be credible by their sponsor. This means that they have demonstrated either *Authority Influence* or *Resource Influence* to a degree that is satisfactory to their sponsor. *Rational Influence* is the ability to influence people to THINK things based largely on their *creativity*. To succeed, minorities must demonstrate *Reputation Influence* or *Thought Influence* to the satisfaction of their sponsors. Finally, *Emotional Influence* is the ability to influence people to FEEL things and is based on their ability to *connect* with people that they are attempting to influence. This means that they have demonstrated *Belief Influence* and *Inspiration Influence* in a way that connects with their sponsors.

It is essential that leaders of organizations, who are committed to increasing the effectiveness of minority employees, work with these employees to answer these four important questions. Minority employees that do not answer these questions and respond accordingly are virtually guaranteed to fail.

SECTION IV

Applying Intelligent Influence

CHAPTER 11
Applying Influence Awareness

Intelligent Influence Exercises

Much of this book has been focused on case studies of corporations and individuals who have consciously or unconsciously applied the *Intelligent Influence* process to achieve extraordinary success. I wrote this final section of the book to enable readers to explore the role of influence in their own lives. The exercises, in this section of the book, are designed to help readers achieve specific goals by increasing their influence within a target group. Those readers who have read the previous chapters now know why the *Intelligent Influence* process is the single most important new approach to leadership development. They are, therefore, in a great position to apply the *Intelligent Influence Framework* to their own careers and businesses.

In the next four chapters, I have included exercises for each of the four steps in the *Intelligent Influence* process. These exercises were developed to provide the hands-on guidance necessary to ensure that individuals, at all levels of an organization, have the *Intelligent Influence* skills they need to achieve their career goals, maximize personal productivity, and increase the effectiveness of project teams. These thought-provoking activities require readers to undertake some intense (but extremely interesting) internal and external reflection. Once people complete them, they will develop a deeper understanding of themselves and their relationships with others. They will most likely want to refer to this section of the book over and over again, throughout their career, to identify ways in which they can strategically increase their influence in a particular situation.

Intelligent Influence Workshops

My hope is that the exercises that follow will help readers personalize the revolutionary new approach to human interaction outlined in *Intelligent Influence: The 4 Steps of Highly Successful Leaders and Organizations*. However, to experience the most benefit from the *Intelligent Influence* process, it is essential to participate in an *Intelligent Influence Workshop* led by a professional, certified to teach this unique leadership development approach. These extraordinary interactive and effective programs are designed to increase participants' *Internal Influence* and *External Influence* in a way that will significantly increase their effectiveness both at home and at work.

Intelligent Influence Groups™

In his book *The Tipping Point*, Malcolm Gladwell discusses the unconventional path to publishing success of author Rebecca Wells. He explains that her book *Divine Secrets of the Ya-Ya Sisterhood* did not become a bestseller until it secured a place as a favorite of women's book groups across the country. The book grew in popularity because of the unique way in which it brought women together, enhanced their interaction, and increased the quality of their lives.

Intelligent Influence is a very different book than *Divine Secrets of the Ya-Ya Sisterhood*. However, the unique way in which it inspires people to think about influence makes group discussion and reflection on the role of influence in life a great deal of fun for both men and women. I continue to be amazed by the very open, honest, and entertaining discussions that take place in the *Intelligent Influence Workshops* that I lead. Conversations about the role of influence in life seem to free people to speak openly and honestly about their influence-driven successes and failures. I, therefore, encourage readers to form an informal *Intelligent Influence Group* comprised of family, friends, or co-workers. I am convinced that members of these groups will have a lot of fun completing the exercises included in this section of the book. In addition, they will enjoy discussing the business cases presented in earlier chapters. *Intelligent Influence Group* members will also derive tremendous personal and professional benefits from the group discussion and sharing of personal experiences.

I define *Influence Awareness* for an individual as "*the process of understanding the most significant ways in which a person has been influenced in the past and the ways in which the person is currently influenced.*" Prior to initiating this step, most people are in a state of *Unconscious Influence Incompetence* where they have no idea about the direct connection between influence and success in life and work. They don't know what they don't know about influence.

The exercises that follow are designed to help you, the reader, develop the *Influence Awareness* skills that you need to negotiate the first step of the *Intelligent Influence* process. To remind you of the relationship between each of the steps of the *Intelligent Influence* process, I provide the *Intelligent Influence Framework* below with the *Influence Awareness* step highlighted:

Intelligent Influence Framework™

	Internal Influence	*External Influence*
Influence Understanding	*Step 1* **Influence Awareness**	*Step 2* **Influence Impact**
Influence Actions	*Step 3* **Influence Management**	*Step 4* **Influence Maximization**

Influence Awareness Exercises

To get the most out of the *Intelligent Influence* exercises in this section of the book, I encourage you to do the following:

1) Get some paper and a pen or pencil.

2) Read each of the exercises and questions.

3) Take some time to think about your answers.

4) Write down your answers so you can refer to (and possibly revise) them at a later date.

5) Once you have completed all the answers, take some time to reflect on each answer. Think about what you have learned and finalize your personal *Intelligent Influence Plan.*

Experienced *Intelligent Influence* trainers have found that this process of writing and reflection is an excellent way to help individuals begin the process of learning how to strategically utilize the principles of influence to achieve extraordinary success. I hope that you enjoy the very thought-provoking questions that follow.

Influence Awareness Exercise #1

Pretend that you were creating the *Influence Hall of Fame*[TM] and you had to choose the first inductees. List the person, product, or company that you think has had the most influence in each of the five categories listed below over the last 100 years. Write down the reasons why you have chosen to induct that person, product, or company into the *Influence Hall of Fame.*

– Leader
– Business Person
– Inventor
– Product
– Company

I like to call *Influence Awareness Exercise #1* the "*Influence Hall of Fame Exercise*[TM]." It is designed to encourage reflection on the role of influence on a person's perception of the world. I have found that this exercise is an excellent way to help people begin the process of understanding the powerful role of influence in history and the world.

Write down the names of five people who influenced you the most during each of the four periods of your life listed below. The influence of these individuals could be positive or negative. Once you have written down the names of the five people in each period, list the reasons why you have chosen these individuals.

#2– Childhood

#3– Ages 13 to 18

#4– Ages 19 to 22

#5– In Your Career

Influence Awareness Exercises #2–#5 will empower you to begin the process of recognizing the influential role that key people have played in your life over the years. These exercises will help you reflect, in a new way, on people who have played an important role in helping you to become the person you are today. We are all standing on the shoulders of others. It is important to identify the people whose shoulders we are standing on to get a clearer picture of the reasons why we think the way we think and do what we do.

Influence Awareness Exercise #6

On a scale of 1-10 (10 being the most influential), how influential (please consider both positive and negative influences) have the following <u>people</u> been in your life?

– Parents

– Siblings

– Other Family Members

– Spouse/Boyfriend/Girlfriend

– Child/Children

– Friends

– Co-workers

– Boss

– Religious or Spiritual Leader

– Anyone Else _____

Influence Awareness Exercise #6 will help you begin to think more broadly about the relative influence of different people in your life. We often take other people in our life for granted. Sometimes we do not think about the important role that they played in our life until we lose them. By thinking about the impact of these people on our life, we get a better sense of how to manage positive influences in our life.

It is easy to overlook the role of non-human influences in our life. *Influence Awareness Question #7* will help you begin the process of identifying the role of these influences in your life. You obviously have greater control over non-human influences than you do over people influences. Therefore, the answer to this question will give you some insight into ways that you can effectively manage the non-human resources in your life. For example, if reading books is not as great an influence in your life as you would like it to be, you can change that by simply taking time to read more.

We are influenced a great deal by the subjects that interest us the most. For example, those people who like politics or sports are influenced to do, think, or say certain things related to their favorite politicians or athletes. *Influence Awareness Exercise #8* will help you begin to think more intentionally about the subjects that interest you the most and influence you to think the way you think, do what you do, and spend time with certain people. Your answers will help you develop a strategy to manage these influences more effectively.

Influence Awareness Questions #2-5 were focused on people who have been influential throughout your entire life. *Influence Awareness Question #9* is intended to help you identify the most influential people in your life today. The answer to this question will help you develop a greater awareness of your influences outside of work today.

Influence Awareness Exercise #10 is intended to help you identify the most influential people in your current place of employment. The answer to this question will help you develop a greater awareness of the ways in which you are influenced at work.

Readers who complete each of the ten *Influence Awareness Exercises* will be prepared to begin Step 2 of the *Intelligent Influence* process where they analyze their *Influence Impact*. In Chapter 12, I provide ten exercises that will help you understand your influence-related developmental needs.

CHAPTER 12

Applying Influence Impact

Influence Impact Exercises

I define *Influence Impact* as "*the process of understanding the most significant ways in which a person, project team, or organization currently influences others and the areas of influence where improvement is needed.*" People initiating this step are in a state of *Conscious Influence Incompetence* where they have become aware that they know very little about their influence strengths and weaknesses. The exercises in this chapter are designed to help you develop the *Influence Impact* skills that you need to negotiate the second step of the *Intelligent Influence* process. To remind you of the relationship between each of the steps of the *Intelligent Influence* process, I provide the *Intelligent Influence Framework* below with the *Influence Impact* step highlighted:

Intelligent Influence Framework™

	Internal Influence	*External Influence*
Influence Understanding	*Step 1* ***Influence Awareness***	*Step 2* ***Influence Impact***
Influence Actions	*Step 3* ***Influence Management***	*Step 4* ***Influence Maximization***

As described in Chapter 2, the foundation of the success of corporations and individuals is the manner in which they utilize six very distinct types of *Intelligent Influences*. These six specific types of influence have often been overlooked by many executives and researchers because they have been buried in the broad concept of "leadership." However, they are the "DNA" of leadership. I provide brief definitions of each of the six types of *Intelligent Influence* below:

The Six Types of Intelligent Influence

Authority Influence = Influence derived from position or ability to command.

Belief Influence = Influence derived by making people believe in the unknown and/or unproven.

Inspiration Influence = Influence derived from the ability to inspire people to act.

Reputation Influence = Influence derived from the broad-based respect of others.

Resource Influence = Influence derived from sharing valuable assets.

Thought Influence = Influence derived from innovative ideas or skills.

One of the most important things individuals must do to begin to maximize their influence is to understand their *Influence Strengths*^{TM} and *Influence Weaknesses*^{TM} based on the six types of *Intelligent Influence*. The exercises in this chapter are designed to facilitate readers' reflection on the influence that they (and others) perceive that they currently have.

Influence Impact Exercise #1

On a scale of 1-10 ("10" being "very often" and "1" being "never"), how often do the following things happen to you at work or at home?

– You are asked for advice.

– You lead meetings/discussions.

– You make people laugh.

– You are asked to manage a project.

– You challenge others to achieve a specific objective.

– You find yourself making the final decision.

– You are asked to speak publicly.

– You receive compliments on your work.

– You ask insightful questions.

– You are asked for help.

The best ways to assess the extent of your influence is to examine the frequency with which you demonstrate each of the six types of *Intelligent Influence*. *Influence Impact Exercise #1* provides a useful way to begin the process of examining the scope and breadth of the influence that you have on others. For example, if you continually receive compliments from co-workers on the quality of your work, then you have significant *Reputation Influence* at work.

Influence Impact Exercise #2 is structured to encourage you to reflect on the extent of your influence both at home and at work. It will help you begin to develop the ability to think deeply about the way in which you are viewed by others. Extraordinarily influential people know how to strategically use positive influence throughout their entire day. It is important to remember that the intelligent use of influence is not something that you turn on or off. It is a learned competency that requires practice 24 hours a day.

Influence Impact Exercise #3

On a scale of 1-10 (10 being "very influential"; 1 being "no influence"), how would you rate yourself on the following?

- Your influence at home
- Your influence at work
- Your influence with your family
- Your influence with your friends
- Your influence with your neighbors
- Your influence at your religious institution (if you have one)
- Your influence in your local community
- Your influence on the internet
- Your political influence
- Other groups_____

It is very easy to ignore the extent of your influence on others. *Influence Impact Exercise #3* should motivate you to honestly assess the extent of your influence in different aspects of your life. Once you complete this exercise, you should take some time to write down the reasons why you have little or no influence with a particular audience. This will help you begin to identify your influence developmental needs and initiate your preparation for the *Influence Management* step.

Influence Impact Exercise #4

Please rate the frequency with which you do the activities listed below using the following scale:

A = I do this as often as I should.
B = I almost do this as often as I should.
C = I am not close to doing this as often as I should.
D = I need to do this less often.
E = Does not apply to me.

– Provide business or personal advice.

– Lead projects/meetings/discussions.

– Write down my thoughts and ideas for others to discuss.

– Make people laugh.

– Help others.

– Find myself making the final decision.

– Challenge others to achieve a specific objective.

– Give compliments.

– Ask insightful questions.

– Speak publicly.

The frequency with which you do certain key things is a very important indicator of the extent of your influence on others. *Influence Impact Exercise #4* is designed to encourage you to reflect both on the influence that you have on other people and the influence they have on you. It will also help you gauge your level of satisfaction with the extent of your influence. The frequency of every one of the activities listed in the exercise is driven by either your ability to influence others or their ability to influence you. Once you have rated each of these activities using the appropriate letter on the scale, you should write down the influence-based reasons that determine the frequency of the activity.

Influence Impact Exercise #5

Using the scale below, rate how often <u>you</u> feel that the following takes place at work. Write down the reasons why you chose a particular number for each question.

5= Almost Daily; 4= Frequently; 3=Occasionally; 2=Rarely; 1=Never

– You utilize your position to exert significant control over the actions of others.

– You use the passionately held viewpoints of a group to motivate them to action.

– You appeal to the senses of others in a way that motivates them to take the actions that you would like them to take.

– People tell you that they have heard wonderful things about you or the quality of your work.

– You exert control over personal resources that others need or want.

– You receive compliments on the uniqueness of your abilities, thoughts, or ideas.

Influence Impact Exercise #5 is designed to encourage you to do an honest self-assessment of your influence strengths and weaknesses. The first item relates to *Authority Influence*; this is designed to determine if you think you have the influence that comes with a powerful position. The second item relates to *Belief Influence*; it is focused on identifying if you think that you are influencing people to believe in a particular project or activity.

The third item relates to *Inspiration Influence*; it is designed to determine whether you think that you stimulate the emotions of others in a way that makes them more productive.

The fourth item relates to *Reputation Influence*; this question is intended to determine if you think that you have a stellar reputation in your organization. The fifth item relates to *Resource Influence*; it is structured to identify if you think that you control valuable resources in the organization. Finally, the sixth item relates to *Thought Influence*; it helps to determine if you think that you have influence related to your innovative ideas, thoughts, or actions.

I am convinced that every organization, at a minimum, should ask each member of their senior management team to complete a self-administered *Influence Impact Assessment*^{TM}. This will ensure that they are cognizant of the role of influence in their success or failure. In addition to the self-administered assessment, extraordinary organizations would have these executives participate in a *360 Influence Impact Assessment*^{TM} where their boss, key co-workers, and subordinates complete the assessment. More often than not, there is a significant difference between the answers to the self-administered questions and those completed by the people they work with. The difference between these answers identifies the developmental (*Influence Management*) needs of the executive. It is amazing how much you learn about a person's effectiveness in an organization when the person, his or her boss, peers, and subordinates complete these questions.

Influence Impact Exercise #6

Using the scale below, rate how often you feel that <u>your peers</u> perceive that the following takes place at work. Write down the reasons why you chose a particular number for each question.

5= Almost Daily; 4= Frequently; 3=Occasionally; 2=Rarely; 1=Never

– You utilize your position to exert significant control over the actions of others.

– You use the passionately held viewpoints of a group to motivate them to action.

– You appeal to the senses of others in a way that motivates them to take the actions that you would like them to take.

– People tell you that they have heard wonderful things about you or the quality of your work.

– You exert control over personal resources that others need or want.

– You receive compliments on the uniqueness of your abilities, thoughts, or ideas.

It is extremely important to assess the extent of your influence on your peers. Far too many professionals do not take the time to think about the manner in which they are viewed by the people they work with. *Influence Impact Exercise #6* will motivate you to think about the ways in which you influence your peers.

Influence Impact Exercise #7

Using the scale below, rate how often you think that the people you supervise would say that the following takes place at work. Write down the reasons why you chose a particular number for each question.

5= Almost Daily; 4= Frequently; 3=Occasionally; 2=Rarely; 1=Never

– You utilize your position to exert significant control over the actions of others.

– You use the passionately held viewpoints of a group to motivate them to action.

– You appeal to the senses of others in a way that motivates them to take the actions that you would like them to take.

– People tell you that they have heard wonderful things about you or the quality of your work.

– You exert control over personal resources that others need or want.

– You receive compliments on the uniqueness of your abilities, thoughts, or ideas.

Many executives think that they have extensive influence on the people that they supervise. They mistakenly assume that people on their project teams love them and will follow them to the ends of the earth. However, when they take the time to reflect on the extent of their influence on the people they supervise, they often realize that their influence may not be as great as they once thought it was. *Influence Impact Exercise #7* facilitates your ability to make an educated guess about the extent of your influence on subordinates.

Influence Impact Exercise #8

Using the scale below, rate how often you feel that <u>your boss</u> would say that the following takes place at work. Write down the reasons why you chose a particular number for each question.

5= Almost Daily; 4= Frequently; 3=Occasionally; 2=Rarely; 1=Never

- You utilize your position to exert significant control over the actions of others

- You use the passionately held viewpoints of a group to motivate them to action.

- You appeal to the senses of others in a way that motivates them to take the actions that you would like them to take.

- People tell you that they have heard wonderful things about you or the quality of your work.

- You exert control over personal resources that others need or want.

- You receive compliments on the uniqueness of your abilities, thoughts, or ideas.

People spend a lot of time trying to please their boss without an influence strategy. They rarely take the time to honestly examine if they are influencing the person they report to in the way that they want to. *Influence Impact Exercise #8* will help you think about your influence strengths and weaknesses in your relationship with your boss. This exercise can potentially help you develop an *Influence Management* strategy designed to influence your boss to recommend you for a raise or promotion.

Influence Impact Exercise #9

Based on your answers to *Influence Impact Exercises #5–#8*, answer the following questions as honestly as possible.

– In which of the types of influence do you excel? Why?

– In which of the types of influence do you need improvement? Why?

– What do you need to do to change the way that others perceive your influence?

Influence Impact Exercises #5–#8 are designed to provide you with a structured way to begin to assess the types of influence where you are strong and weak. *Influence Impact Exercise #9* will help you initiate the process of identifying your influence developmental needs. It should also help you outline a strategy to increase your influence in key ways.

Please complete the following statement and rank in order the statements, where "1" is the goal you would most like to accomplish and "6" is the goal you would least like to accomplish.

I would like to be . . .

– considered the most innovative thought leader in the company.

– an employee with control over valuable company resources.

– the most respected employee in the company.

– able to motivate my peers and subordinates to do what they are uncomfortable doing.

– a person with the ability to rally co-workers around a common goal.

– someone with a larger span of control.

Influence Impact Exercise #10 is structured to help you begin to identify your influence priorities. You are forced to rank your influence goals to help you prioritize the action steps that you need to take to get the influence that you desire. You may find that you want to accomplish many of the goals listed in the exercise. However, placing them in rank order will help you initiate the process of *Influence Management* in a more structured and deliberate way.

CHAPTER 13

Applying Influence Management

Influence Management Exercises

I define *Influence Management* as "*the intentional effort by a person, group, or organization to utilize a developmental plan designed to strategically increase their External Influence.*" People initiating this step are in a state of *Conscious Influence Competence* where they have undertaken the process of managing influences in their life to achieve success. They know how to increase their influence; however, they are not yet ready to do it instinctively.

The exercises in this chapter are designed to help you develop the *Influence Management* skills you need to negotiate the third step of the *Intelligent Influence* process. To remind you of the relationship between each of the steps of the *Intelligent Influence* process, I provide the *Intelligent Influence Framework* below with the *Influence Management* step highlighted:

Intelligent Influence Framework™

	Internal Influence	External Influence
Influence Understanding	*Step 1* **Influence Awareness**	*Step 2* **Influence Impact**
Influence Actions	*Step 3* **Influence Management**	*Step 4* **Influence Maximization**

Influence Management Questions

The ten exercises that follow are based on self-assessments of the reader's personality, skills, *External Influence* goals, and *Internal Influence* plans. This relationship is depicted in the *Individual Influence Management* equation in the box below:

Individual Influence Management

Personality Type (P) + Skills (S) + Internal Influence (I) = External Influence (E)

Where the symbols represent the following:

P = The personality type of an individual.

S = The skills and abilities a person possesses.

I = The developmental influence action (training, coaching, team building, etc.).

E = The ways in which this person influences others as a result of actions.

The *Influence Management Exercises* in this chapter are a useful tool designed to help you begin the process of thinking more broadly about the relationship between the influences in your life and your goals, skills, and personality. Completing the exercises is the first step in managing the influences in your life. At first, some of these exercises may not seem relevant to you. However, in combination, they will help you undertake deep reflection on each element of the *Individual Influence Management* equation. Please answer the exercises that follow as honestly as you can.

On a scale of 1-5 (using the scale below), indicate how closely you identify with each personality trait.

5 = *You strongly identify with the trait.*
4 = *You identify with the trait.*
3 = *You occasionally identify with the trait.*
2 = *You don't identify with the trait.*
1 = *You have the opposite trait.*

– Introvert

– Realist

– Risk-Averse

– Detail-Oriented

– Intuitive

– Pensive

– Visionary

– Logical

– Judgmental

– Other(s)

Feel free to expand the list of personality traits in *Influence Management Exercise #1.* My hope is that these traits will help you identify some additional traits that represent key aspects of your personality. If you have taken a personality assessment recently, include traits from that instrument. It is essential that you have a very good understanding of your personality to fully benefit from the *Influence Management* process.

Influence Management Exercise #2

On a scale of 1-5 (using the scale below), indicate how closely you identify with each skill.

5 = This skill is one of your major strengths.
4 = You believe that you have this skill.
3 = You have this skill in certain circumstances.
2 = You don't have this skill.
1 = This is a weakness.

– Writing

– Critical Thinking

– Computer Programming

– Research

– Sales

– Finance

– Engineering

– Presentation

– Negotiation

– Other(s)

In *Influence Management Exercise #2,* I have listed some of the skills that play an important role in a person's success at work. Please feel free to expand the list of skills. Unfortunately, very few people take the time to honestly assess what their skills and weaknesses are in a structured way. They often assume that they have certain skills. However, frequently these skills become rusty and weaken over time. It is, therefore, extremely important to identify your skills and weaknesses on a regular basis so you have a good sense of your current development needs.

On a scale of 1-5 (using the scale below), indicate how closely you identify with the *External Influence* goal listed below:

5 = You strongly identify with the goal.
4 = You identify with the goal.
3 = This is a low-level goal.
2 = You don't identify with the goal.
1 = You have no interest in the goal.

– Enhance one of the six types of *Intelligent Influence.*
– Become a CEO.
– Manage a project team more effectively.
– Get a promotion/change careers.
– Make more money.
– Report to a different boss.
– Develop a unique skill.
– Find a new job.
– Write a book.
– Other _____

If you don't know where you want to go, you will never be able to develop a plan to get there. This is true in both vacation travel and career success. I have included just a few of the possible *External Influence* (career) goals you may want to pursue. As you can see, some of these are extremely difficult goals while others are significantly less challenging. Please feel free to customize the list in *Influence Management Exercise #3* so that it better fits with your professional and personal goals.

On a scale of 1-5 (using the scale below), indicate how closely you identify with the *Internal Influence* plan listed below:

5 = This is the most important part of your plan.
4 = This is part of your plan.
3 = This is a possible part of your plan.
2 = This is not a part of your plan.
1 = This would never be helpful to you.

– Work more closely with a mentor or sponsor at work.

– Consult with an executive coach.

– Attend a specific training program.

– Pursue a business certification.

– Get a college/graduate degree.

– Transfer to another division.

– Write a personal business plan.

– Start a business.

– Participate in a corporate workshop.

– Other _____

The only way to effectively manage influence is to understand your personality, skills, and *External Influence* goals. Hopefully, *Influence Management Exercises #1-#3* helped you develop a deeper understanding of these three key components of influence management. *Influence Management Exercise #4* is structured to enable you to identify the *Internal Influence* action steps that you need to achieve your particular *External Influence* goals. Please add to this list as you see fit.

> ### *Influence Management Exercise #5*
>
> Write down five key aspects of your personality (introvert, extrovert, decisive, optimistic, sensitive, risk-averse, innovative, etc.) and explain how these traits either help or hinder your performance at work.

Influence Management Exercises #1–#4 were designed to provide you with a high-level introduction to *Influence Management.* You should now have a general understanding of each of the elements of the *Individual Influence Management* equation. The next few exercises are designed to help you explore each of the elements of the equation and their connection to your performance at work. *Influence Management Exercise #5* will help you examine the relationship between your personality and success or failure at work.

> ### *Influence Management Exercise #6*
>
> Write down five of your most valuable work skills (critical thinking, writing, computer programming, research, engineering, finance, negotiation, conflict management, etc.) and explain how these traits impact your performance at work.

In *Influence Management Exercise #2,* you began the process of identifying your skills. Hopefully, you now have a good idea of your key skills and abilities. *Influence Management Exercise #6* will help you undertake a deeper exploration of your skills and their connection to your performance at work.

Influence Management Exercise #7

Write down your five most important *External Influence* goals (get a promotion, make more money, manage a larger team, start a business, etc.) and explain why these goals are important to you.

In *Influence Management Exercise #3,* you began the process of identifying your *External Influence* goals. *Influence Management Exercise #7* will help you do a more thorough job of identifying your *External Influence* goals.

Influence Management Exercise #8

Based on your answers to *Influence Management Exercises #5-#7,* write down the five *Internal Influence* action steps (training, executive coaching, additional education, identification of mentors and sponsors, etc.) that you need to take to accomplish your *External Influence* goals and explain why these action steps are important to you.

In *Influence Management Exercise #4,* you began the process of identifying your *Internal Influence* plans based on your personality, skills, and *External Influence* goals. *Influence Management Exercise #8* will help you develop a comprehensive list of the *Internal Influence* action steps necessary for you to achieve your *External Influence* goals.

The exercises in this chapter are structured to help you understand the process of outlining a comprehensive *Influence Management* plan. I have discovered that the most effective way to develop this plan is to write down your planning process, in detail, before you begin this extraordinarily rewarding process. As always, it is extremely important to "plan your work and work your plan." *Influence Management Exercise #9* will help you begin this important process.

To experience the benefits of *Influence Management* (and reach the stage of *Conscious Influence Competence*), you must be able to understand the relationship between *Intelligent Influence* and success at work. *Influence Management Exercise #10* is structured to facilitate your exploration of this relationship. Once you are able to effectively utilize *Influence Management*, you are ready to begin the process of attaining *Influence Maximization* as outlined in Chapter 14.

CHAPTER 14

Applying Influence Maximization

Influence Maximization Exercises

I define *Influence Maximization* as "*the process of maximizing influence with a targeted group of people.*" The ultimate goal in this step is to reach the stage of *Unconscious Influence Competence* where you instinctively maximize influence, in every situation, involving significant human interaction. The exercises in this chapter are designed to help you develop the *Influence Maximization* skills you need to negotiate the fourth and final step of the *Intelligent Influence* process. To remind you of the relationship between each of the steps of the *Intelligent Influence* process, I provide the *Intelligent Influence Framework* below with the *Influence Maximization* step highlighted:

Intelligent Influence Framework™

	Internal Influence	*External Influence*
Influence Understanding	*Step 1* **Influence Awareness**	*Step 2* **Influence Impact**
Influence Actions	*Step 3* **Influence Management**	*Step 4* **Influence Maximization**

The exercises that follow were designed to help you develop the *Influence Maximization* skills you need to complete the *Intelligent Influence* process. The exercises are based on analyzing *Behavioral Influence*, *Rational Influence*, and *Emotional Influence*. This relationship is depicted in the *Caldwell Spheres of Influence* diagram and each of the spheres is defined in the box below the diagram:

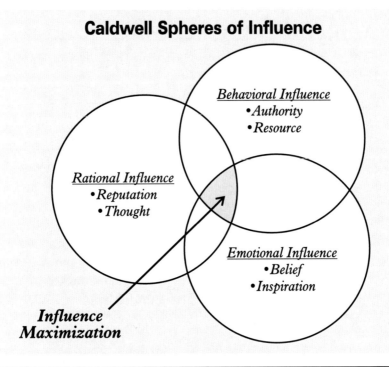

Caldwell Spheres of Influence

- *Behavioral Influence*
  - *Authority*
  - *Resource*
- *Rational Influence*
  - *Reputation*
  - *Thought*
- *Emotional Influence*
  - *Belief*
  - *Inspiration*

Influence Maximization

Caldwell Spheres of Influence

The Behavioral Influence sphere is often referred to as the "Sphere of Credibility." It is defined as "the ability to influence people to <u>do</u> things and is comprised of Authority Influence and Resource Influence."

The Rational Influence sphere is often referred to as the "Sphere of Creativity." It is defined as "the ability to influence people to <u>think</u> things and is comprised of Reputation Influence and Thought Influence."

The Emotional Influence sphere is often referred to as the "Sphere of Connection." It is defined as "the ability to influence people to <u>feel</u> things and is comprised of Belief Influence and Inspiration Influence."

The sharing of "best practices" is one of the most effective tools utilized
by management consultants to support their recommendations to clients.
The best consultants are able to provide detailed examples of successful
approaches used by other companies and explain why a similar approach
would benefit their client. These examples help to make clients feel
comfortable that this approach has the potential to be successful. For
many of the same reasons, you will find tremendous value in examining
Influence Maximization best practices. *Influence Maximization Exercise
#1* will motivate you to identify examples of people who have utilized
Behavioral Influence best practices to be successful. These individuals have
strategically used *Authority Influence* and/or *Resource Influence* to achieve
specific goals and objectives.

The purpose of *Influence Maximization Exercise #2* is to encourage you
to identify examples of people who have utilized *Rational Influence* as a
best practice. These individuals have strategically used *Reputation Influence*
and/or *Thought Influence* to achieve specific goals and objectives.

> ### *Influence Maximization Exercise #3*
>
> Write down the names of three to five people who have effectively used the *Emotional Influence* sphere. Describe how they have successfully utilized this sphere of influence.

The purpose of *Influence Maximization Exercise #3* is to encourage you to identify examples of people who have utilized *Emotional Influence* as a best practice. These individuals have strategically used *Belief Influence* and/or *Inspiration Influence* to achieve specific goals and objectives.

> ### *Influence Maximization Exercise #4*
>
> Write down the names of three to five people who have effectively used all three of the *Caldwell Spheres of Influence*. Describe how they have successfully utilized all three of these spheres simultaneously.

The purpose of *Influence Maximization Exercise #4* is to encourage you to identify examples of people who have utilized each of the three *Caldwell Spheres of Influence*, in combination, as a best practice.

Influence Maximization Exercises #5–#7 are designed to provide insight into ways to maximize *Behavioral Influence*, *Rational Influence*, and *Emotional Influence*. To maximize your influence, others must be convinced that you have the ability to effectively "produce an effect without the direct exercise of command." The following 30 questions are designed to help you determine the areas of influence-based leadership where you excel, as well as, those areas that you need to work on to increase your influence. Please answer the questions below as honestly as possible. We recognize that some of the questions may seem repetitive; however, throughout this section of the book, we have attempted to reframe and reposition similar questions in a way that will ensure that each complete self-assessment is as accurate as possible.

Influence Maximization Exercise #5

Please answer the following questions (using the numerical system below) about the two types of influence that comprise the sphere of *Behavioral Influence*. During your workday, how often do you . . .

5 = Almost Daily; 4 = Frequently; 3 = Occasionally; 2 = Rarely; 1 = Never

Authority Influence

– assign projects to others?

– set a clear vision, mission, and goals for the group you have authority over?

– utilize your formal or informal authority to exert control over the actions of others?

– use your position to remove obstacles that prevent co-workers from achieving specific goals?

– find yourself publicly understating the extent of your power in an organization?

Resource Influence

– share your resources in a way that produces the most benefit for others?

– exert control over resources that others need or want?

– use your contacts, assets, or resources to help others accomplish specific goals?

– take full advantage of the personal or work resources that you have access to?

– strategically use your contacts, assets, or work resources for a public social good?

Your answers to *Influence Maximization Exercise #5* will give you additional insight into the extent of your *Authority Influence* and *Resource Influence*. If you find that you rarely do many of the activities listed, you should create an *Influence Development Plan* that provides the *Internal Influence* that you need to enhance your ability to strategically utilize *Authority Influence* and/or *Resource Influence*.

Influence Maximization Exercise #6

Please answer the following questions (using the table below) about the two types of influence that comprise the sphere of *Rational Influence*. During your workday, how often do you . . .

5 = Almost Daily; 4 = Frequently; 3 = Occasionally;
2 = Rarely; 1 = Never

<u>Reputation Influence</u>

– serve in a leadership role because of your reputation as a successful leader?

– take time to manage your public image?

– make sure that your successes are visible to a broad audience?

– write articles/blogs, speak publicly, or appear on videos/ TV, etc.?

– hear from others that they were told good things about you?

<u>Thought Influence</u>

– present your innovative ideas in a simple, focused, and easily understood way?

– use your intellect to help others achieve their goals?

– clearly explain how a person can benefit from using your unique idea in accomplishing an important objective?

– utilize available data to convince others to support or act on your innovative ideas?

– provide evidence why your ideas or thoughts are original and likely to be successful?

Your answers to *Influence Maximization Exercise #6* will give you additional insight into the extent of your *Reputation Influence* and *Thought Influence*. If you find that you rarely do many of the activities listed, you should create an *Influence Development Plan* that provides the *Internal Influence* that you need to enhance your ability to strategically utilize *Reputation Influence* and/or *Thought Influence*.

Influence Maximization Exercise #7

Please answer the following questions (using the table below) about the two types of influence that comprise the sphere of *Emotional Influence*. During your workday, how often do you . . .

5 = Almost Daily; 4 = Frequently; 3 = Occasionally; 2 = Rarely; 1 = Never

Belief Influence

– actively involve others in the development of concepts that will lead to a common way of thinking?

– find yourself taking time to ensure that others' beliefs are aligned with yours?

– use commonly held views or beliefs to motivate others to action?

– connect colleagues' beliefs to clearly defined action steps?

– find yourself speaking publicly about the common beliefs of your project team?

Inspiration Influence

– intentionally connect what you are requesting or saying with people's desires, hopes, values, and dreams?

– convince people in an enthusiastic manner to do what you would like them to do?

– provide a clear and compelling vision of the things that can be accomplished with the support of others?

– generate passion in the people you are speaking to by appealing to their competitive spirit?

– appeal to co-worker's positive self-worth and pride in accomplishing a task or achieving a goal?

Your answers to *Influence Maximization Exercise #7* will give you additional insight into the extent of your *Belief Influence* and *Inspiration Influence*. If you find that you rarely do many of the activities listed, you should create an *Influence Development Plan* that provides the *Internal Influence* that you need to enhance your ability to strategically utilize *Belief Influence* and/ or *Inspiration Influence*.

If you have taken the time to answer most of the questions in this section of the book, you are ready to begin to think tactically about using the *Intelligent Influence* process to address specific challenges both at work and at home. *Influence Maximization Exercise #8* asks two very critical questions about your strategy to effectively use influence to overcome a specific challenge. Your answers to these questions will help you develop an *Intelligent Influence* guided road map to success.

The single most significant factor in determining a person's salary and promotion opportunities is the extent of the person's influence on sponsor(s). It is, therefore, essential that you develop a plan to utilize *Intelligent Influence* in a way that will help you influence a sponsor to support your promotion or raise. In much the same way, small businesses looking for venture capital or bank loans must effectively influence a sponsor to enable them to get what they want. The purpose of *Influence Maximization Exercise #9* is to help you develop this important plan.

If you have read *Intelligent Influence: The 4 Steps of Highly Successful Leaders and Organizations* in its entirety, completed each of the exercises in this section of the book, and practiced using influence strategically (both at work and at home), you will be able to demonstrate *Unconscious Influence Competence* by intuitively utilizing influence to achieve your goals. The influence development process, presented in this book, will help you increase your *Intelligent Influence Quotient* (IIQ) and serve as the foundation of your success in any endeavor involving human interaction. You will know that you have reached a state of superior influence competence in business when you are able to complete *Influence Maximization Exercise #10* with little or no difficulty.

The unique approach to human interaction presented in this book is applicable to many different aspects of life. The *Intelligent Influence* process is successful because people, around the world, respond to influence in remarkably similar ways. From business to government, from nonprofits to politics, from parenting to religion, *Intelligent Influence* promises to rewrite the rules of how we communicate and move each other to transform the world. I wish you success in your efforts to intelligently use influence to achieve your personal and professional goals.

BIBLIOGRAPHY

Blanchard, Ken and Johnson, Spencer. *The One Minute Manager*. New York: William Morrow, 1981.

Brandt, Richard L. *One Click: Jeff Bezos and the Rise of Amazon*. New York: Penguin, 2011.

Carnegie, Dale. *How To Win Friends and Influence People*. New York: Pocket Books, 1936.

Cherniss, Cary, and Daniel Goleman. *The Emotionally Intelligent Workplace*. San Francisco: Jossey-Bass, 2001.

Cialdini, Robert B. *Influence Science and Practice*. Boston: Pearson Education, 2009.

Cohen, Allan R., and David L. Bradford. *Influence without Authority*. Hoboken: John Wiley & Sons, 2005.

Collins, Jim. *Good To Great*. New York: HarperCollins, 2001.

Covey, Stephen R. *The 7 Habits of Highly Effective People*. New York: Simon & Schuster, 1989.

Drucker, Peter F. *The Practice of Management*. New York: Harper & Row, 1954.

Ferrazzi, Keith, and Tahl Raz. *Never Eat Alone*. New York: Doubleday, 2005.

Friedman, Thomas L. *The World Is Flat: A Brief History of the Twenty-First Century*. New York: Farrar, Straus and Giroux, 2005.

Gabler, Neal. *Walt Disney: The Triumph of the American Imagination*. New York: Random House, 2006.

Girard, Joe. *How To Sell Anything To Anybody*. New York: Fireside, 1977.

Gladwell, Malcolm. *Blink*. New York: Little, Brown and Company, 2005.

Gladwell, Malcolm. *Outliers*. New York: Little, Brown and Company, 2008.

Gladwell, Malcolm. *The Tipping Point*. New York: Little, Brown and Company, 2000.

Goleman, Daniel. *Emotional Intelligence*. New York: Bantam, 1995.

Goodwin, Doris Kearns Goodwin. *Team of Rivals: The Political Genius of Abraham Lincoln*. New York: Simon & Schuster, 2005.

Katz, Donald R. *Just Do It: The Nike Spirit in the Corporate World*. Holbrook: Adams Media Corporation, 1994.

Kroeger, Otto, Janet M. Thuesen, and Hile Rutledge. *Type Talk at Work: How the 16 Personality Types Determine Your Success on the Job*. New York: Tilden Press, 2002.

Lewis, Michael. *Moneyball*. New York: WW. Norton & Company, 2003.

Machiavelli, Niccolo. *The Prince*. Ontario: Prohyptikon, 2009.

Maxwell, John C. *The 17 Indisputable Laws of Teamwork: Embrace Them and Empower Your Team*. Nashville: Thomas Nelson, 2001.

Maxwell, John C. *The 21 Irrefutable Laws of Leadership: Follow Them and People Will Follow You*. Nashville: Thomas Nelson, 1998.

Merriam-Webster. *Merriam Webster's Dictionary*. Springfield: Merriam-Webster Incorporated, 2001.

Pendergrast, Mark. *For God, Country, and Coca-Cola: The Definitive History of the Great American Soft Drink and the Company That Makes It*. New York: Basic Books, 1993.

Peters, Thomas H., and Robert H. Waterman. *In Search of Excellence: Lessons from America's Best Run Companies*. New York: HarperCollins, 1982.

Porter, Michael E. *Competitive Strategy: Techniques for Analyzing Industries and Competitors*. New York: Simon & Schuster, 1980.

Ries, Al, and Jack Trout. *The 22 Immutable Laws of Marketing*. New York: HarperBusiness, 1994.

Sherrow, Victoria. *Encyclopedia of Hair: A Cultural History*. Westport: Greenwood Press, 2006.

Smith, Adam. *The Wealth of Nations*. New York: Simon & Brown, 2012 (original copyright 1776).

Stanley, Thomas J., and William D. Danko. *The Millionaire Next Door*. Lanham: Taylor Trade Publishing, 1996.

Strasser, J.B., and Laurie Becklund. *The Unauthorized Story of Nike and the Men Who Played There*. New York: Harcourt Brace Jovanovich, 1991.

Tzu, Sun. *The Art of War*. London: Oxford University Press, 1963.

Ziglar, Zig. *Zig Ziglar's Secrets of Closing the Sale*. New York: Berkley Books, 1984.